Photography in focus

Photography in focus

A BASIC TEXT

MARK JACOBS
KEN KOKRDA

NATIONAL TEXTBOOK COMPANY • Skokie, Illinois 60076

ACKNOWLEDGMENTS

Sharon Savage, Elaine Equi, Chicago Art Institute, Yosef Karsh, Jerry Uelsmann, Paul Caponigro, W. Eugene Smith, R. Bruce Duncan, Tim Basaldua, Leonard Fiddle, Kaye Lucas, Bonnie Pullman, Barbara Simons, Rich Mandich.

INTRODUCTION

It's a visual world we live in today, and the camera is making an impact on our lives as it never has before. Cameras are in the hands of doctors, lawyers, business executives, educators—people in every walk of life. And though photography might not play an essential role in their careers, it is an integral part of their approach to those careers, and to their lives.

Because photography is a tool that can unlock your creativity, make you see yourself and your world in a very special way, and communicate that special insight to others, learning to use this tool can help you to lead an enriched life.

Popular Photography is most pleased to cooperate in the publishing of this carefully thought-out text, *Photography in Focus,* as part of its continuing national program to increase public awareness of the value of photography in education and in everyday life. The book you hold in your hands is your key, not just to learning a valuable skill, but to opening the door to a more satisfying life.

Sidney Holtz
Popular Photography

Contents

Photograms

The word "photography" comes originally from two Greek words that mean "light drawing." Light is the heart of photography, from the initial exposure of the picture to the final developing and printing.

The easiest photographic image to make is the photogram, a simple record of light and shadow. The photogram was also the earliest surviving example of a negative-positive image relationship. The calotypes, or "photogenic drawings," made in the early 19th century by William H. F. Talbot were essentially photograms.

A photogram is a recorded shadow. It can be made by two methods, one using direct sunlight and the other using darkroom equipment.

Printed-Out Photogram

A "printed-out" photogram does not require darkroom or chemicals. A kind of printed-out photogram can be seen in a suntan —the darkening of skin that is exposed to the sun's rays, while the "unexposed" part of the skin remains light. In a photographic photogram, the pattern is caused by the action of light on a sheet of photographic paper. Photographic paper has a coating or "emulsion" on one side that is sensitive to light. Exposing the paper to direct sunlight for a few hours causes the emulsion side of the paper to turn dark.

To make a printed-out photogram, simply take a sheet of photographic printing paper (such as Kodak's Kodabromide®, Velox®, Ilford's Ilfrobrom® or other manufacturers' equivalent products) and lay some objects on the emulsion side (shiny side). You might use keys, coins, leaves, matches, or any other opaque objects. Since you will be working out of doors with sunlight (which is brighter than electric light), you may want to lay a sheet of glass over lightweight objects to hold them still. The objects should remain in place on the emulsion side for at least one hour. This period of time, during which the paper faces the sun, is called the "exposure."

composing the photogram

printed-out photogram

The finished picture will show the objects' shadows as white, while the portion of the paper that was exposed to the sun has turned dark. The objects blocked the sun's rays from hitting portions of the light-sensitive paper, while the other portions were exposed, thus causing those areas to darken. Since the image is white where the light was blocked off and dark where the light struck it, it reverses the tonal scale and thus produces a "negative" image.

There is one major problem in making a photogram by the direct sunlight method. Unless the print is somehow stabilized or "fixed" by using a chemical called hypo or fixer, it will continue to be affected by light until the whole image eventually turns dark.

When a photogram is made in a darkroom, using chemicals, including a fixer, the image is more lasting and less likely to fade in light; this method is more flexible. Three photographic chemicals are used: a developer, a stop bath, and a fixer. Again, objects are placed on a sheet of photographic paper which has not been exposed or opened previously in any kind of light except a darkroom safelight. Lay your objects on the emulsion side of the paper. Keep in mind that the more transparent an object is, the more light will pass through it, causing the area underneath the object to turn darker.

After you arrange the objects on the paper in a pleasing composition, turn on a white light (roomlight) for two seconds. (Make sure you've put away the paper not being used.) Remove the objects from the paper. At this point you will notice that nothing seems to have happened to the paper. It is still white, seemingly unaffected by the two-second exposure. However, an invisible image has been recorded on the sensitized paper. Called the "latent image," it must be chemically treated or "developed out."

The chemical used to bring out the image is called the developer. A developer chemically changes the latent or invisible image on the emulsion to a visible image composed of minute particles of metallic silver. The paper should remain in the tray of developer solution for about two minutes. While the paper is in the developer, you must continue to work in light that is safe for the paper, because it is still sensitive to normal light.

Each processing step is labeled with the chemical, recommended time in the chemical, and the action required during the recommended time. Grey background indicates safe light illumination. All chemicals and wash water should be the same temperature.

developer
2 minutes
agitate

stop bath
1 minute
agitate

hypo
See manufacturer's instructions
agitate

water
20 minutes
agitate

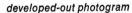

developed-out photogram

The next chemical, the stop bath, stops the action of the developer. It is a mild acid solution, and so the paper should remain in the tray of solution for no longer than a minute, or else the image will be stained. After it has been immersed in this solution, the image stops developing. However, it remains light-sensitive until it is immersed in the third chemical solution, the hypo fixer.

The fixer removes the unused sensitized material from the light, unexposed areas of the photogram. After it has been immersed in the fixer for about one minute, the photogram is no longer sensitive to light and can be viewed in room light. The print remains in the fixer for no longer than 10 minutes since, like the stop bath, fixer contains acid, and after several hours the image will be bleached out.

After the print leaves the fixer, it must be washed for about 30 minutes in running water to remove the excess hypo. If this is not done, the print may start to stain after several months, due to certain ingredients in the fixer.

Next, the photogram must be dried. The quickest way is simply to wipe off the excess water with a clean sponge and air dry the print; however, it will curl. If time allows, put the print between two blotters and press a heavy book on top to keep the print flat. With this method, it usually takes about two days for the print to dry thoroughly. The best method, if the equipment is available, is an electric dryer, which will dry the print in about ten minutes.

A photogram made by the printed-out method can also be made light permanent. Immerse the print in the fixer for five to ten minutes and then wash and dry it as described above.

After both prints have dried, compare them. Notice that the print made by the "printed-out" method has an unpleasant yellow-brownish cast and lacks the brilliance of the "developed-out" photogram.

Negative–Positive Relationship

Both these methods of making photograms produce *negative* images; in other words, they reverse the normal tonal scale, substituting white for black. There are two methods, the wet process and the dry process, that can be used to reverse the negative image to a normal positive.

The advantage of the wet process is that the negative photogram does not have to be dried before a positive is made. After a negative photogram has been washed in running water for ten minutes, turn the safelight on and the room light off. Take a sheet of unexposed photo paper and put it in the wash water for two minutes. Remove both the wet negative and the wet unexposed paper and press them together, emulsion sides facing each other. Lay the paper flat with the negative image on top. After that, remove the excess water by running your hand over the back of the paper.

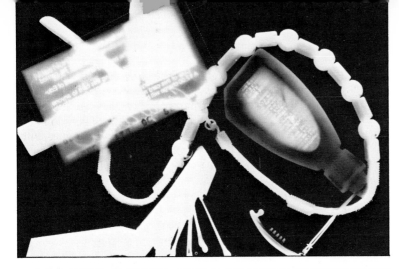

negative photogram

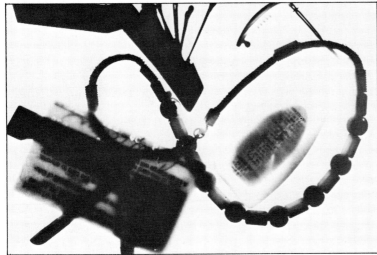

positive photogram

Then turn on the room light (white light) for one second. Develop the fresh paper in the same manner as you did the first. If the positive image is too light, increase the time that you leave the room light on. If the positive is too dark, shorten the exposure time.

To make a positive after the negative has been dried, place a clean piece of glass on top of the two sheets to ensure close contact between the negative and the unexposed paper. Again, work under safelight conditions. Make sure that the negative is on top. Expose the paper to room light as before and then develop the image.

Photograms offer a unique way of expression. Experiment with different shapes and sizes of objects. After you learn the technique

photogram of transparent objects

photogram drawn with penlight

of photograms, try using objects that are not completely opaque. These will add different tones of grays in your photograms instead of stark black-and-white silhouettes. You may also want to try varying your light source—for instance, use a small flashlight instead of an overhead light. The effects that can be achieved add another dimension to the photograms. Photograms have only one limitation, your imagination.

Assignment: Photograms

1. Make at least two photograms by the printed-out method. One photogram should be made with opaque objects (sticks, leaves, bottle caps, weeds, torn cardboard, etc.) and the other with transparent objects (plastic, glass, etc.).
2. Make at least two successful photograms using the developing-out method. One should use both transparent and opaque objects; the other can use any sort of objects you prefer, but some of them should be moved during the exposure. What effect does moving the objects have on the photogram image?
3. Make positive prints (at least two) of your best negative photograms.

photogram of pieces of paper

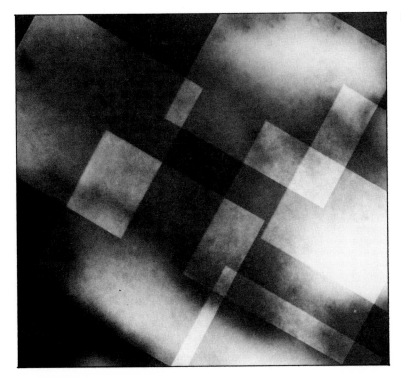

The Pinhole Camera 2

A camera is often compared to the human eye. Both a camera and the eye are enclosed chambers with an opening that allows light to enter the dark chamber from the front and then pass through a lens. Both have a light-sensitive area behind the lens.

The lens in both the camera and the eye serves the same function—to gather the rays of light from the scene being viewed and then transmit them, in an expanding cone, back to this light-sensitive area. In the eye, this light-sensitive area is called the retina; in a camera, it is the film.

In both the eye and the camera, a device in the lens controls the amount of light transmitted. In the eye, this device is a muscle called the iris. In the camera, the device is called the iris diaphragm. Both the eye and the camera work best when there is a moderate amount of light—too little light, and the details cannot be seen, while too much light is blinding.

Both the camera and the eye must be focused on a scene, or the image will be blurred. In the eye, the lens, controlled automatically by the brain, focuses the light rays on the retina. The brain also "translates" the image on the retina into something meaningful. In the camera, the lens focuses the image.

The one very important difference between your eye and a camera is that the camera has no intelligence of its own—no "brain" to control it. Camera manufacturers try to make cameras easier to use by installing electrical circuitry that will make instantaneous calculations of the picture-taking situation, and equipping them with digital read-outs much like a calculator. Yet no camera, no matter how new or how expensive it is, can see for you. The camera serves the photographer; it is not the master. The camera is the photographer's paintbrush, the film is the paint, but only the eye can see the painting. The earliest forerunner of the camera—the *camera obscura*—did not use a lens to form the image. "Camera obscura" is Latin for "dark room" (or "chamber"), and at first it was simply that, a dark room with a small hole in one of the walls. People sitting inside the room could see fuzzy images from the outside form on the white wall opposite. The image of the camera

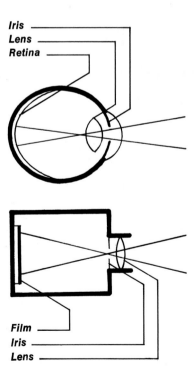

Iris ──
Lens ──
Retina ──

Film ──
Iris ──
Lens ──

obscura was formed by unfocused light rays, and the sharpness of the image depended on the size of the hole in the wall and the distance between the hole and the opposite wall. A large hole and a long distance combined to produce a blurred image. But because a small hole meant a faint image, the camera obscura without lenses had to compromise between sharpness and brightness.

According to most historians, the camera obscura began to be equipped with lenses about the 16th century, making possible the development of portable models with a sharper, brighter image. However, one very simple type of camera still made today does not have a lens. Using the basic principle of the camera—light entering a dark chamber and producing an image—it is called the "pinhole camera."

How to Make a Pinhole Camera

The first thing needed to make a pinhole camera is a box that can be made light-tight so that no stray rays of light will enter and fog the film or photographic paper. Boxes that can be used for this purpose are shoeboxes, oatmeal boxes, or any similar box that has a tight-fitting lid and will hold a 4 inch by 5 inch sheet of photographic paper.

Next, you need to make the pinhole, which will serve as the lens on the camera. Take a smooth piece of aluminum foil about an inch square. Lay it on a flat, hard surface such as metal or glass and press only the top or point of a needle straight down through the foil. The hole should be perfectly round and free from ridges, and the foil should not be pushed out where the pinhole was made. The hole itself will be hard to measure, but it should be too small for the entire pin to fit through.

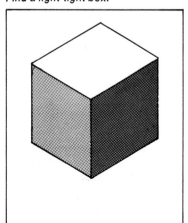

Find a light-tight box.

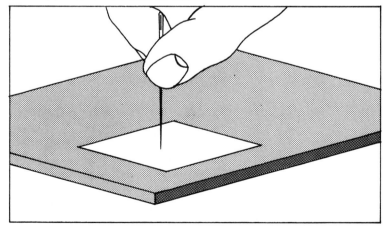

Carefully puncture the aluminum foil.

After you have selected the box, paint the inside of it flat black. If the inside remains a light color, it will reflect or bounce the light passing through the pinhole in all directions and fog your paper. Next make a hole in the center of one side of the box and tape the aluminum foil with the pinhole securely over the larger hole, using an opaque tape such as black electrical tape or masking tape. Make sure that the pinhole is in the center and then take another piece of opaque tape and cover the pinhole. This piece of tape will act as the shutter of your camera.

Loading the pinhole camera with photo paper must be done in darkroom conditions using a safelight. Use an unexposed fresh sheet of photo paper, like that used in making the photograms, and center it on the side opposite the pinhole. Make sure that the emulsion side is facing the hole. After this is done, tape the four corners down so that the paper won't move around inside the box. (See center illustration on the right.) Replace the lid on the box and you are ready to take a picture.

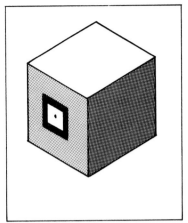

Tape aluminum foil over square hole.

Taking the Pinhole Picture

"Exposure" in photography can mean two things: (1) the actual taking of the picture and (2) the time that light is allowed to enter the light-tight camera. For instance: "Elaine *exposed* 13 pictures today, each one having an *exposure* of two minutes. Luckily for her, it was a bright day—otherwise her *exposure* would have been eight minutes each and she couldn't have *exposed* as many pictures."

To take a picture (or *expose* a picture) with a pinhole camera, place it on a firm support such as a table, a windowsill, a rock, or a chair. Tape or weight it so it won't move accidentally. This is important, as any movement during the exposure will cause your picture to be blurry and out of focus. After your camera has been securely fastened to the support, open the tape that is covering the pinhole. Expose the picture for two minutes if it's very sunny outside, for about eight minutes if it's cloudy bright. You must then develop your picture in the darkroom as you did the printed-out photogram. The resulting image will, of course, be a negative. Making a positive is done in the same manner as with a photogram. If your negative is too light, then increase your exposure time. If your negative is too dark, shorten the exposure time. Just remember that the brighter it is outside, the shorter your exposure time should be; while the darker it is, the longer your exposure time will be.

You may want to make three or four pinhole cameras so that you'll be sure of getting the correct exposure. With Camera #1 make an exposure of two minutes, with camera #2 a four-minute exposure, with camera #3 a six-minute exposure, and so on. This procedure is called "bracketing" the exposure.

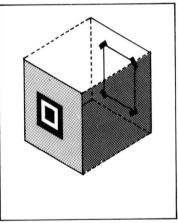

Tape pinhole closed and position photo paper.

Secure box with heavy object; remove tape and expose.

Movement (or lack of it) is the main consideration in choosing subjects for pinhole camera pictures. Most people can't sit still for a two- to eight-minute exposure; they move and cause a blurry image. It is best to shoot unmoving subjects like landscapes, buildings, or trees.

There are actually four variables that affect the exposure time: (1) the sensitivity of the paper or film to light; (2) the size of the pinhole; (3) the pinhole-to-paper distance; and (4) the lighting conditions.

All photographic papers and films are sensitive to light. However, some kinds of film and paper are more sensitive than others. In general, film is more sensitive to light than paper. Therefore, after you learn about film development (Chapter 4), you may want to use film instead of paper in your pinhole camera, especially if you intend to photograph something other than a still-life.

The size of the pinhole also affects the necessary exposure time. A small hole, of course, will allow less light to pass through it, while a larger hole will allow more light to enter. Then, why not just make a bigger pinhole? The reason is that many more rays of light will pass through the larger hole, and because there is no way to guide them, they will record themselves over a much larger and less well-defined spot of the paper or film. What about using a more sensitive film and a smaller hole to get a sharper picture? This would work if it were not for the effect of diffraction. Diffraction refers to the scattering of light rays as they pass close to any edge. As the hole is made smaller, the proportion of scattered rays of light to unscattered rays increases, thus, also producing a less defined image. In short, a pinhole camera cannot ever produce as clear or sharp a picture as a camera with a lens.

The shorter the distance from a pinhole to the paper (or film), the shorter the exposure time can be. Conversely, the longer the pinhole-to-paper distance, the longer the exposure necessary.

Another factor of distance produces an optical effect that you may want to use in your picture-taking. A camera in which the pinhole-to-paper distance is substantially less than the diagonal measurement of the paper will produce a small image that includes a wider field of view. For example, the diagonal measurement of a 4 x 5 inch sheet of paper is about 6½ inches. If you put a 4" x 5" sheet of paper 2 inches from your pinhole, you'll get a "wide-angle" effect. That is, more area will be shown in your picture because the subject and its surroundings will be reduced in size.

Conversely, if the pinhole distance to the paper is much greater than the diagonal measurement, the image will be magnified to look so much greater in size than it really is. This is called a "telephoto" effect. If the pinhole-to-paper distance is about the same as the diagonal measurement, the effect will be "normal,"—that is, about what your eye would see within the same space from the same distance as the camera.

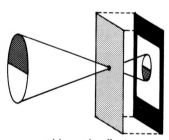
wide-angle effect

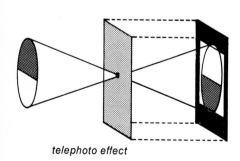
telephoto effect

The last factor that determines exposure is the amount of light. The more light, the shorter the exposure time. The less light there is, the longer the exposure time. Bracketing the exposure by making several pinhole cameras and photographing the same scene under the same lighting conditions with different exposures will help you in getting a properly exposed picture.

Other Simple Cameras

Of the cameras made today, the closest to the pinhole camera are the box camera and the Instamatic® type. The important difference is that these cameras have a lens.

Most roll film cameras have seven basic parts: (1) a light-tight box to keep out light and serve as a frame to hold other parts; (2) a lens or lenses to guide light to the film; (3) a lens opening to control the amount of light that reaches the film; (4) a shutter to control the amount of light that reaches the film; (5) a trigger to release the shutter; (6) a knob or lever to advance the film; and (7) a viewfinder to look through and frame the picture.

1 *light-tight box*
2 *lens*
3 *adjustable lens opening*
4 *adjustable shutter speed control*
5 *shutter release*
6 *film advance lever*
7 *viewfinder*

The frame in many inexpensive cameras is made out of plastic. In better quality cameras, the frame is metal, which, of course, is stronger and more durable. The frame is designed so that other parts may be attached to it without destroying its light-tight body.

Lenses in cameras vary in quality. However, they all serve the same purpose, which is to focus the light rays that pass through them onto the light-sensitive film. Lenses in most Instamatic-type cameras are made of plastic. Better quality lenses are usually made of glass, which can be polished to a much finer degree and so produce a sharper image. The pinhole camera has no lens to focus the light rays to a common point. Because the pinhole lacks a lens the image it produces lacks sharpness.

The lens opening of a camera controls the amount of light that reaches the film, as does the pinhole in your camera. Usually in an Instamatic-type camera, the opening also remains the same size. However, more sophisticated lenses usually have diaphragms that can change the hole size. This diaphragm works much like the iris in your eye, which adjusts the size of your pupil to let in more or less light.

While the lens opening controls the *amount* of light that reaches the film, the shutter of a camera controls the *time* that light is permitted into the dark chamber. The piece of tape that was used to open and close the opening of the pinhole camera was its shutter. Most inexpensive cameras have shutters that cannot vary in speed. Thus, if there is not enough light available, the resulting picture is usually underexposed (too dark). In better cameras, the shutter speed can vary from very fast (1/2000 of a second) to slow (1 second).

The shutter release in both a box camera and a more sophisticated camera is simply a button that releases the shutter so that light can enter the camera.

Your pinhole camera allowed for taking only one picture at a time without the camera being reloaded. This, of course, would be impractical for most photographers. A film advance lever or knob moves the film through the camera, thus making it possible to take many pictures on one roll of film.

So that the photographer can "see" what the picture will include, a viewfinder is built into most cameras. This allows the photographer to frame and compose his or her photographs. In some types of cameras, called the single-lens reflex, the photographer is able to look right through the lens.

Assignment: The Pinhole Camera

1. Construct two pinhole cameras as described in the chapter. One camera should have a pinhole-to-paper (or film) distance that is at least twice as long as the other.
2. Load each camera with a piece of photographic paper. Cut a small notch in the top of the paper before you load it in the

camera. Remember that all loading and unloading of your camera must be done only under a darkroom safelight.

3. Expose each piece of film according to the times recommended in Chapter 3. You may have to make several exposures to get a good one, since the exposure times given are only estimates. Keep a record of all your exposure times, along with the lighting conditions at the time you made each exposure.

4. After you have developed all your exposed pinhole camera pictures, select those you judge to be most properly exposed. (To keep track of your exposure times, it is a good idea to determine in advance what exposure time you are planning to use and write this time lightly in pencil on the back of the paper before you load it in the camera.)

5. Remember that you cut a notch in the top of your paper before it was exposed. After development, notice where the notch is in relationship to the top and bottom of your picture. From this part of the experiment, what can you conclude about how cameras form images?

6. How can you explain the difference in image size in the pictures formed by the two cameras? What does this tell you about the effects of pinhole-to-paper distance?

7. Are the best exposures from each camera of equal length, or did the pictures from one of your cameras require more or less time than the other to get an equal exposure? What does this tell you about the relationship between exposure time and pinhole-to-paper distance?

8. Now enlarge the size of the pinhole in one of your cameras and expose two or three more pictures under the same lighting conditions as your first set of pictures. Keep track of your exposure times again.

9. Develop the set of pictures made with the camera with the enlarged pinhole. What do the results tell you about the effect of the size of the pinhole (or lens opening) on exposure time?

10. Make some positive prints from your best pinhole negative pictures. Use both the wet and dry methods described in Chapter 1.

Using the Adjustable Camera

Introduction

Photographic film is a cornerstone of photography. However, unless this light sensitive material is loaded correctly into a camera, photography becomes an exercise in futility. There is only one way to load film into your camera, the right way.

Loading the Film

The easiest type of film to load is the cartridge used in Instamatic®-type cameras. Simply drop the cartridge in a position where it lies flat inside the camera back. The cartridge will fit in only one way, so that loading it upside down is impossible for most people. Close the back of the camera firmly until it locks and advance the film by moving the winding mechanism until it stops. This usually takes about one-and-a-half turns of the lever or knob. On the back of the camera is a window that shows you how many pictures you have taken. Since cartridge loading is simple, there are only two things to remember: (1) turn the advance lever or knob after each picture until it stops (don't force); and (2) after the last picture has been made on the roll, advance the film until no more paper can be seen in the window.

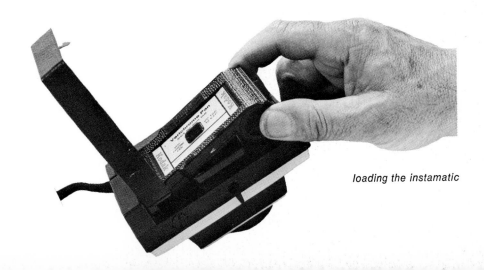

loading the instamatic

Rich Mandich

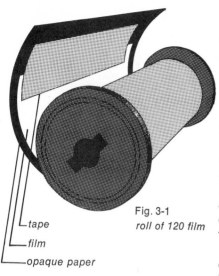

Fig. 3-1
roll of 120 film

tape
film
opaque paper

Roll film is a term for film that is rolled on a spool rather than enclosed in a magazine (as is 35mm film) or in a cartridge (as is Instamatic® film). (See Fig. 3-1.) Like cartridge film, roll film has an opaque paper backing. Loading it into the camera requires that the full spool be inserted into an empty chamber in the back of the camera. (See Fig. 3-2a.) After the spool is firmly in position, draw out some of the tapered paper leader and insert that tapered end into the slot of the take-up spool. Make sure that the tapered end is caught in the slot, or else the film will not be pulled through the camera. (See Fig. 3-2b.) Close the back of the camera and turn the advance lever until the window shows #1. This is the usual method in roll film cameras. However, some cameras are equipped with automatic stopping devices so that watching the window for each consecutive exposure is not necessary. Check your camera manual to be sure.

Another method of film loading is used for 35mm film, which comes in a magazine in lengths of either 20 or 36 exposures. (See Fig. 3-3.) There is no paper backing on 35mm films, which means that (1) after all the pictures have been taken, the film must be rewound back into the magazine or cassette; and (2) there is no

Fig. 3-2a
insert film into empty chamber

Fig. 3-2b
insert paper into take-up spool slot

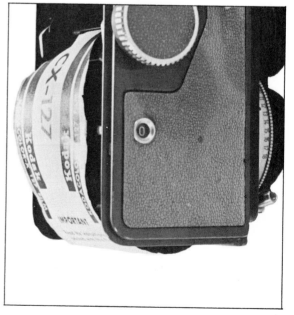

window on a 35mm camera to show how many pictures you have taken. Instead, there is a film counter numbered from 0 to 36.

There are six steps in loading 35mm film into the camera. (See Fig. 3-4a–f.) First, open the back cover of the camera. In some cameras this is done by pulling up on the rewind knob until the lock is released on the back. Other 35mm cameras have a separate latch which must be released before the back will open.

Second, insert the film cartridge, or cassette, into the specially designed chamber. With most 35mm cameras it is necessary to lift up the rewind knob to do this. After the cassette is secure in the chamber, push the rewind knob back down. This action will prevent the cassette from moving around inside the camera. Third, draw out some of the tapered film leader from the cassette and insert it into the slot of the film take-up spool. Make sure that the film leader is placed so that the bottom edge is resting evenly on the edge of the take-up spool. After checking this, advance the film by using the advance lever, making sure the film perforations engage the sprockets on both sides. Don't worry about losing pictures because the back is open. Film manufacturers always supply extra film in the cartridges for this situation. (Some photographers

Fig. 3-3
a 35mm cassette

Fig. 3-4a
open back

Fig. 3-4b
insert cassette

Fig. 3-4c
insert tapered leader into take-up spool slot

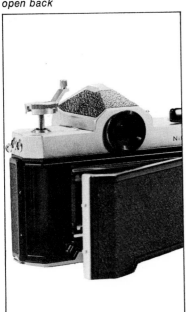

Fig. 3-4d
engage film perforations with sprockets

Fig. 3-4e
turn rewind crank clockwise to take up slack

Fig. 3-4f
advance film and release the shutter until frame "one" is indicated

may brag that they can take 39 pictures on a 36-exposure roll. But what they don't mention are how many rolls they have ruined by trying to squeeze in those extra exposures.)

After you have made sure that the sprockets of the take-up spool are sticking through the perforations of the film, close the back of the camera until it locks. Then, after the back is closed, turn the rewind crank slowly in a clockwise direction until you feel the tension. Don't force the rewind crank, as it can rip the perforations of the film. The purpose is to take up any slack in the film; since a 36-exposure roll is almost five feet long, there will usually be some slack. Advance the film by turning the lever. Depress the shutter release button and advance again until the number 1 appears in the exposure counter window. While you are advancing the film, watch the rewind knob. It should rotate counterclockwise, indicating that the film is advancing through the camera properly.

When the entire roll of film has been exposed, you must rewind the film back into the cassette before opening the camera. Locate the rewind button on the camera and depress it. By doing this you release the gears inside the camera so that the film can be rewound without ripping the perforations. After the button has been depressed, turn the rewind crank clockwise until you feel the tension release. Open the back of the camera and remove the film cassette.

One word of advice: After you have taken 20 pictures on a 20-exposure roll or 36 on a 36-exposure roll, rewind the film back into the cassette. Don't try to sneak another picture on the roll. You may win out, but you may rip the end of your film to shreds. It just doesn't pay.

Focusing Methods

Your eyes are constantly focusing and refocusing as they "see" a subject. If your eyes focus improperly and you wear glasses, then you know how blurry things look without them. This gives you a good idea of how a camera will record subject matter if it is not focused properly.

There are at least five basic systems of focusing found in different types of cameras: (1) non-adjustable; (2) estimation of distance and "zone-focus"; (3) rangefinder; (4) twin-lens reflex ground glass; and (5) single-lens reflex.

In a non-adjustable camera, there is no device on the lens to control focus. These cameras are set at the factory to be in acceptable focus at a distance of around 10 feet. Usually as long as the subject isn't closer than 6 feet or farther away than 15 feet from the camera lens, the image will look sharp. Pictures taken with these types of cameras at too close a range are unrecognizable blurs.

If the lens on a camera can be moved to compensate for changes in distance, but has no device to see the actual focusing, then the

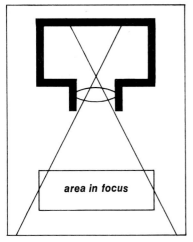

area in focus

non-adjustable

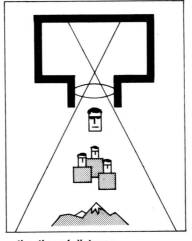

estimation of distance

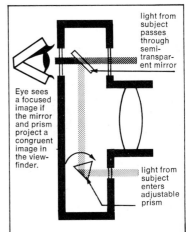

light from subject passes through semi-transparent mirror

Eye sees a focused image if the mirror and prism project a congruent image in the viewfinder.

light from subject enters adjustable prism

rangefinder system

photographer must estimate the distance. This second method ranges from pure guesswork ("That looks like about 6 feet, so I'll set the scale there") to a zone-focus scale on the camera. The scale for zone focus usually shows three or four drawings. If your subject is between 3 and 5 feet away, the scale will show a picture of head and shoulders, which corresponds to that approximate distance. For subjects between, say, 6 and 15 feet away, you would set the scale to the focusing picture of the group scene. Anything beyond 15 feet is "infinity," and thus the focusing scale would be set on a mountain scene. Cameras with slightly finer scales may have settings for close-ups (about 4 feet), for medium shots (up to about 8 feet), for groups in a background (to about 17 feet), and for distance or infinity, such as shots of scenery. Both the zone focusing and the non-adjustable focusing cameras supply only relative sharpness. However, even just estimating the distance is better than having a camera with no means of focusing.

typical rangefinder camera

A rangefinder is an opto-mechanical device that produces two images in the viewfinder of the camera. One image is usually tinted a light color (yellow or red) for better visibility. To bring the camera into focus, rotate the lens until the two images coincide with each other. A rangefinder allows you to see the actual focusing of the lens. Rangefinder cameras are usually 35mm. (There are some Instamatic-type cameras with rangefinders on the market, as well as larger formats.)

The twin-lens reflex method of focusing is used in many larger roll film cameras. These cameras have two lenses, one for focusing and the other for exposing the film. The lenses are attached to the camera so that they move simultaneously. (See Fig. 3-5.) A mirror installed at a 45° angle behind the upper lens reflects the image onto a "ground glass" where the photographer can see it. A hood over the ground glass keeps out strong light and makes the image easier to see. Sometimes a magnifying glass is built into the hood for more critical focusing. In this type of focusing, the camera is held about waist level (the other ways of focusing are usually done at eye level) and the photographer looks down into the hood.

The single-lens reflex (SLR) is the most common method of focusing more sophisticated cameras, whether they use cartridge, 35mm, or roll film. A single-lens reflex camera allows one to view a subject through the actual picture-taking lens. A single-lens reflex camera works much like its older cousin, the twin-lens reflex. (See Fig. 3-6.) A mirror is placed behind the actual picture-taking lens at a 45° angle. The light that forms the image comes through the lens and is reflected upward by this mirror to a viewing screen or ground glass. Then it passes through a prism which turns the image right side up and right side around and delivers that image to the eye. The type of ground glass used determines the manner

Fig. 3-5
twin-lens reflex (TLR)

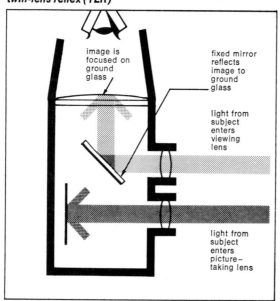

image is focused on ground glass

fixed mirror reflects image to ground glass

light from subject enters viewing lens

light from subject enters picture-taking lens

Fig. 3-6
single-lens reflex (SLR)

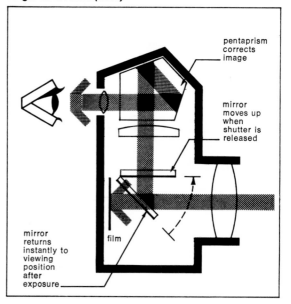

pentaprism corrects image

mirror moves up when shutter is released

mirror returns instantly to viewing position after exposure

film

of focusing. Although there are many modifications in the various types of ground glass used, they generally fall into two categories: split-image and microprism.

A split-image screen or ground glass is one in which the subject is divided into halves. The idea is to restore the image so that the top half does not overlap the bottom half of the screen. In using this type of screen, it is helpful to find a straight line to focus on somewhere in the scene.

The other type of screen found in today's single-lens reflex cameras is the microprism. A microprism screen consists of many small dots that cause the image to appear shimmering where it is out of focus. As the image is focused, the pattern will phase out until the dots are no longer visible. The image is then in correct focus.

Parallax

All cameras except the single-lens reflex and the view camera (which will be discussed in Chapter 11) have viewfinders that are separate from the actual picture-taking lens. Although the distance between the lens and the viewfinder may be only one or two inches, it does create a problem: you see one image through the viewfinder, while your camera lens "sees" the same scene from a slightly different angle. This problem increases as you get closer to the subject. For example, you may be puzzled to find that someone's head has been cut off in a picture when you know you saw it in the viewfinder.

To counteract parallax, some viewfinders, especially those with rangefinders, are marked off with corners. The entire image you want should be framed within these corners. Check your camera's viewfinder to see if there is a built-in parallax correction. If there is none, then just become aware of the problem and learn to compensate for it.

Film Exposure

As you learned by using the pinhole camera, "exposure" is the length of time that the film receives light after it has passed through the lens and shutter of the camera. In an adjustable camera, the photographer manually controls the amount of light that reaches the film. A "correct" exposure is the amount of light needed to produce a usable image upon the film. *Overexposure* results when too much light has been allowed to reach the film. *Underexposure* occurs when too little light comes through.

As you know, the two devices on the camera that control the amount of light that strikes the film are the shutter and the aperture, or lens opening. The size of the opening is usually referred to as the *f*-stop.

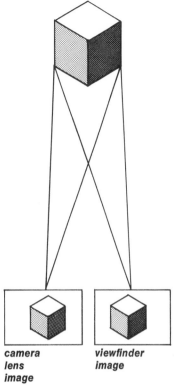

camera lens image   *viewfinder image*

The difference in angle of view is not critical when focusing on distant subjects.

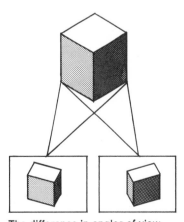

The difference in angles of view increases as the distance between subject and camera decreases. Each lens sees a different part of the subject.

Shutter & Shutter Speeds

There are different types of shutters built into cameras. In the single-lens reflex, the most common type of shutter is an opaque piece of cloth or metal that moves across the lens opening at a predetermined speed, thus controlling the length of time that light falls on the film. This type of shutter is called a "focal plane" shutter, since it is located in the back of the camera where the light rays are focused, that is, where the "picture" or image is formed on the film. The device for setting the shutter speed on a camera with a focal plane shutter is usually located on the top or front of the camera. In some cameras, mainly those with rangefinders, the shutter is located within the lens housing of the camera and so is called a "between-the-lens" shutter.

In the pinhole camera, the exposure could vary between 2 and 8 minutes, so that a difference of 30 seconds did not change the image much. However, photographic film is much more sensitive to light than photographic paper. Because of this, the necessary exposure time to produce a correctly exposed negative is more critical, more precise, and usually shorter. Thus, shutter speed is usually measured in fractions of a second, rather than in minutes. The shutter speeds ordinarily found on today's cameras are expressed as 100, 500, 250, 125, 60, 30, 15, 8, 4, 2, 1 and B. Each of these numbers represents a fraction of a second. For example, a shutter speed indication of "4" means 1/4 of a second; a shutter speed of "250" means 1/250 of a second, and so on. A shutter speed of 1/30 second allows twice the amount of light to reach the film as does 1/60. The speed of 1/60 permits about twice as much light to enter as 1/125. Similarly, by selecting 1/125 over 1/250, you allow twice the light to reach the film. Conversely, using the speed 1/500 instead of 1/250 means that only half as much light will reach the film. The setting of 1/500 is twice as fast as 1/250, and therefore only allows half as much time for light to enter. In other words, using a faster shutter speed lets in only half the light that the next slower speed does; and conversely, the slower shutter speed permits twice as much light to enter as the next fastest speed.

"B" is the only exception; it is a variable speed. When the dial controlling the shutter speed is set at the "B" (for "bulb") position, the shutter remains open for as long as the shutter-release button is depressed. This position is used only for long exposures (called "time exposures") such as are used when photographing the stars at night. Under normal conditions, a shutter speed slower than 1/30 is not common because the normal vibrations of a hand-held camera cause a blurred picture at slower speeds. A rigid support, such as a tripod, is necessary when slow shutter speeds are used.

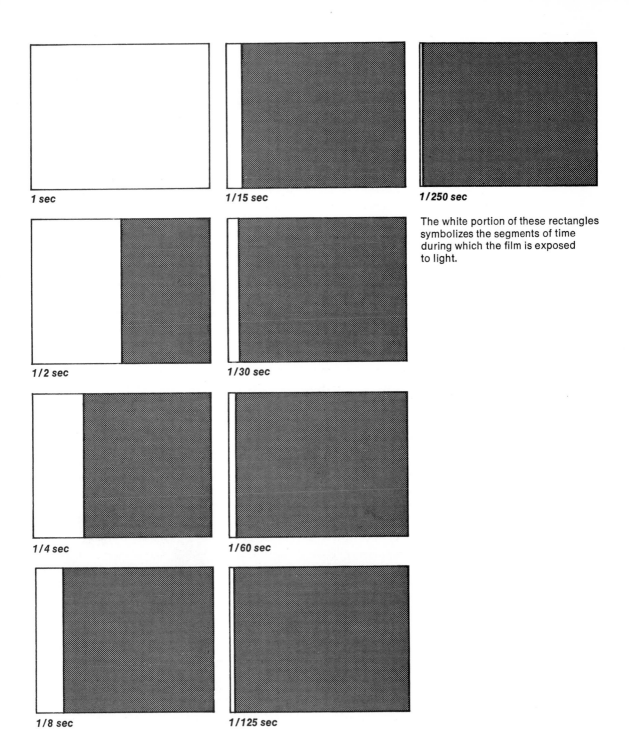

1 sec

1/15 sec

1/250 sec

The white portion of these rectangles symbolizes the segments of time during which the film is exposed to light.

1/2 sec

1/30 sec

1/4 sec

1/60 sec

1/8 sec

1/125 sec

F-Stops

The f/stop diameters illustrated below are exaggerated in order to emphasize the increase in diameter as the f/stop number is decreased.

The second device used to control light in a camera, the *f*-stop, is the opening (aperture) or hole in an adjustable iris diaphragm which controls the amount of light that passes through the shutter and onto the film. (See Fig. 3-7.) This diaphragm is very much like the iris that controls the size of the pupil of your eye. You can see the pupil getting larger or smaller as more or less light strikes it. Try this experiment: Look into a mirror in a dim light. You will see that the opening (the pupil) is rather large in order to let in as much light as possible. Then turn on a bright light, and you will see the pupil suddenly getting smaller as the iris automatically adjusts the opening to the brighter light. Some cameras with an automatic exposure system adjust the opening in the diaphragm automatically when the amount of light changes. On a manual or adjustable camera, the *f*-stop must be set by the photographer. This setting is often made with the "*f*-stop ring," which is usually located around the lens housing of the camera.

There are usually six or seven *f*-stop positions on an adjustable camera lens, each designating an opening of a different size. Some common *f*-stop numbers are 16, 11, 8, 5, 6, 4, 2.8, 2. The large

Fig. 3-7

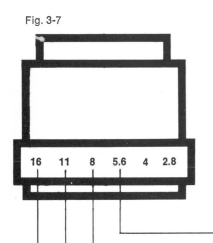

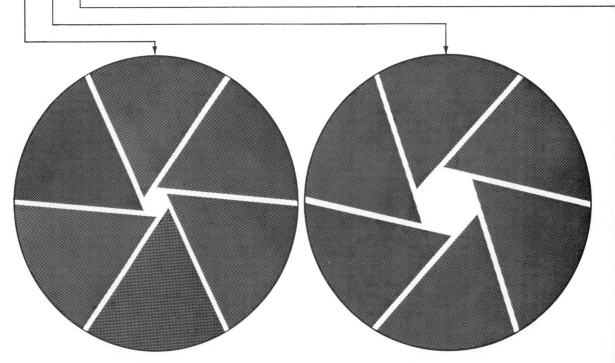

f-numbers produce small lens openings, and the small f-numbers produce large lens openings. This may be confusing at first, but remember that each f-number is really a fraction: since ⅛ is smaller than ¼, an f-stop of "8" is smaller than an f-stop of "4". The numbers used to designate the f-stops and the corresponding lens openings they produce may not seem to fall into any regular order or relationship, because the f-numbers express the ratio between the diameter of the lens and the focal length of the lens. What is most important to understand, though, is that f/1.8 lets in more than twice as much light as f/2.8. Similarly, f/2.8 allows twice as much light to pass through the lens at f/4, and so on down the line. Conversely, f/16 allows only half as much light to enter the lens as f/11, while f/11 permits only half as much light as f/8. In other words, opening the lens by one f-stop permits twice as much light to pass through the lens. By opening the lens two stops, four times the amount of light will reach the film. Closing the lens down a stop allows only half as much light to reach the film. This is the same correlation that exists between the shutter speeds. It is also important to understand that on a lens of any focal length, when focused on infinity, delivers proportionately equal amounts of light to the film.

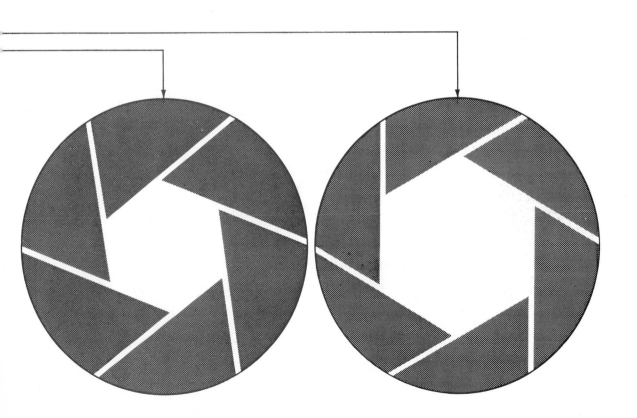

Fig. 3-8

typical hand-held meter

Using a Light Meter

A light meter, or exposure meter, is an instrument that measures the amount of existing light and determines which combinations of shutter speed and f-stop the photographer may use to produce a correctly exposed negative. A light meter may be built into the body of a camera or may be a separate, hand-held device.

Using a Hand-Held Meter. To use any light meter, you must first set the meter to correspond to the type of film you are using. To do this find the ASA dial on the meter. (See Fig. 3-8.) The ASA of a film is the rating in numbers of the film's sensitivity to light. It is printed either on the box in which the film is packed or on the information sheet the manufacturer provides. To learn how to set the ASA number, refer to the operating manual of the meter you are using.

Now hold the meter in the palm of your hand so that the cell of the meter is pointing toward the subject to be photographed. This is called a "reflected" light meter reading because it measures light that is bouncing back from the subject being photographed. This initial reading is indicated by the needle on the dial. With most meters you will be using, you must then align the needle with a marking inside the window of the meter to find the range of correct f-stop/shutter speed settings.

Each combination on the meter yields the same exposure to the negative, but the combination that will work best for you depends upon the subject you're shooting and the effect you want to create. For instance, if you are shooting someone running, and the reading is the same one as shown in the illustration, choosing a shutter speed of 1/125 with an f-stop of 2.8 would "freeze" the subject. However, if you wanted to achieve a blurred effect showing motion, you would use the combination of ⅛ at f/11 so that the shutter would remain open for a longer period.

Using a Built-In Meter. Many newer cameras incorporate a light meter. There are three different classifications of cameras with built-in meters. In one, the meter may be built on the camera, usually on the top. These meters work in the same manner as hand-held meters. After the reading has been made, the photographer transposes the f-stop reading from the meter to the f-stop ring of the camera. The same procedure is necessary to determine and set the shutter speed.

The most popular built-in meter is the "integrated" type. An integrated light meter is controlled by changing either the shutter speed of the camera or the f-stop ring. The important difference between the hand-held meter and the integrated meter is that when using the integrated meter either the shutter speed is selected before the f-stop is known, or the f-stop is known before the speed has been selected. The two factors are not selected in combination as with a hand-held meter.

After you have selected the shutter speed, hold the camera's viewfinder up to your eye and look through it. Inside the viewfinder is a marking, usually a backward *c*, that the needle is to be matched with. (Another type of marking may be a circle that the needle should center on. Check your instruction book.) With the camera still held up to your eye, rotate the *f*-stop ring until the needle inside the viewfinder is centered on the backward *c*. If the needle will not center, the shutter speed is either too fast or too slow for existing light conditions. Rotate the shutter speed ring until the needle inside the viewfinder is centered.

averaging meter

On the newest types of camera, especially 35mm single-lens reflex cameras, integrated light meters have been placed behind the picture-taking lens. Different models of these "through-the-lens" meters read light from different areas of the picture. Therefore, check the instruction manual of your camera to see what area your meter is reading. There are basically three different types of through-the-lens metering systems.

center-weighted meter

The average meter "reads" the entire picture area. This type is useful for most picture-taking situations. The spot meter reads a small area of the picture, usually 10 percent. With such a meter, it is especially important to know the area that is most critical in your photograph. The center-weighted meter is a combination of the spot and averaging meters. Many photographers tend to plan their subject in the center of the photograph; and this meter gives them that exposure calculation without ignoring the rest of the photograph.

spot meter

The third type of built-in meter, the "automatic," sets either the shutter speed or the *f*-stop automatically after the desired lighting is chosen. (In some cases the automatic meter governs both the the shutter and *f*-stop, so that the photographer has no control over the exposure. This type of meter is not very useful for learning the basics of exposure calculation.) Using an automatic camera that allows the photographer to control the shutter speeds is similar to using a camera with an integrated light meter. First, set the ASA dial on the camera. Then select the shutter speed, being sure that the camera is in the automatic position for the *f*-stop. If it is not, your light meter will not work. Then hold the camera to your eye and look through the viewfinder. You will see an *f*-stop scale printed inside the viewfinder, as well as a needle indicator that will point to an *f*-stop. If the needle is above the largest *f*-stop, adjust the shutter to a slower speed. Increase the shutter speed if the needle is below the smallest opening. The camera will automatically use whatever *f*-stop number the needle points to.

If the camera is one that pre-selects the shutter speed, the procedure is the same except that the *f*-stop is chosen first. In this case, the light meter will indicate what shutter speed is to be used.

If the photographer wishes, he can take the camera off "automatic" after he knows what *f*-stop to use. To do this, simply leave

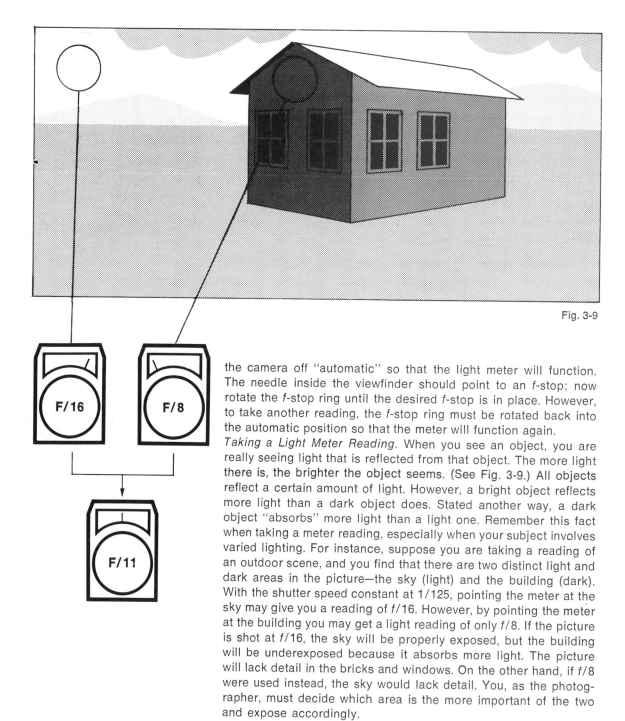

Fig. 3-9

the camera off "automatic" so that the light meter will function. The needle inside the viewfinder should point to an f-stop; now rotate the f-stop ring until the desired f-stop is in place. However, to take another reading, the f-stop ring must be rotated back into the automatic position so that the meter will function again.

Taking a Light Meter Reading. When you see an object, you are really seeing light that is reflected from that object. The more light there is, the brighter the object seems. (See Fig. 3-9.) All objects reflect a certain amount of light. However, a bright object reflects more light than a dark object does. Stated another way, a dark object "absorbs" more light than a light one. Remember this fact when taking a meter reading, especially when your subject involves varied lighting. For instance, suppose you are taking a reading of an outdoor scene, and you find that there are two distinct light and dark areas in the picture—the sky (light) and the building (dark). With the shutter speed constant at 1/125, pointing the meter at the sky may give you a reading of f/16. However, by pointing the meter at the building you may get a light reading of only f/8. If the picture is shot at f/16, the sky will be properly exposed, but the building will be underexposed because it absorbs more light. The picture will lack detail in the bricks and windows. On the other hand, if f/8 were used instead, the sky would lack detail. You, as the photographer, must decide which area is the more important of the two and expose accordingly.

Remember that light areas will force you to "stop down" the lens or force you to use a faster shutter speed, while dark areas

30

exposed at f/22 *exposed at f/8* *exposed at f/11*

Fig. 3-10
Meter the backlight and subject light. Average the two meter readings and expose.

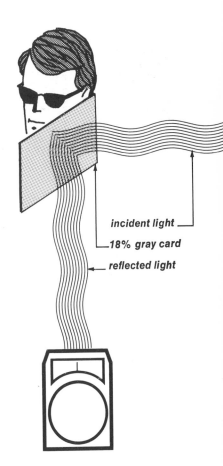

incident light
18% gray card
reflected light

will do just the opposite. Become aware of light and dark areas in your picture by practicing meter readings.

Average Light Meter Readings. Unless you know exactly what effect you want, you may decide to average several meter readings together. In the example just given, the proper sky setting was f/16, while the proper tree reading was f/8. The "average" reading would be f/11, the f-number that falls between the two.

Averaging is also useful when photographing a subject in front of a window. (See Fig. 3-10) This is called "backlighting," because the light behind the subject is stronger than the light reflecting from the subject's face. If you stand back from the subject a few feet and take a meter reading, the meter will be affected by the light behind the subject. For instance, at this point your meter may now produce a reading of f/22. If you took the picture at this f-stop, the subject would be underexposed; that is, it would be silhouetted. If you walk up to the subject and take a reading of his face, the meter may give you a reading at f/8. If this is the stop you use, the effect would be a properly exposed face surrounded by pure white, because the window would be overexposed. However, if you average the two f-stops, using between f/11 and f/16, you will save detail both in the window and in the face.

Sometimes an 18-percent gray card is useful to determine the correct exposure. An 18-percent gray card has a medium-gray surface that reflects 18% of the light that reaches it and absorbs 82% of the light. When held in the position of the subject and read with a reflected light meter, it will (on the average), give the correct reading for calculating exposure.

Power Supplies for Meters. The two types of exposure meters available are the selenium cell meter and the cadmium sulfide (CdS) meter. The CdS meter is powered by a small battery; almost all integrated light meters are of this type. The selenium cell meter does not use a battery for its power. Instead, as light hits the photoelectric cell on the meter, a small amount of electricity is generated and swings the needle indicator over the face of the dial. The more light available, the more power the meter receives, making the needle move further across the dial. A third type of exposure meter is being developed which uses silicon cells, similar to a solid state electrical system. As of yet, however, no cameras have built-in silicon cell meters.

Assignment: Using the Light Meter

1. Find an outdoor area to photograph. Take and record light readings in the bright sunny areas and in areas of shadow. How much variation is there? Express this variation in terms of f-stops.

   Photograph the area using both of the readings taken above. Can you predict what differences will appear in the two negatives? Explain why.

   Make a third exposure of the same situation. This exposure should produce maximum detail in both the highlight and the shadow areas. Explain how you determined this exposure.

2. Find a "backlit" situation to photograph (for instance, a person in front of a window inside a building on a bright day). What settings does the exposure meter give as an average reading? Photograph the scene at one of these settings. Now read the light behind the person and photograph the scene at this setting. Take a light reading of the light falling on the person only. At what distance should you do this? Photograph the entire scene at this new light reading.

3. Practice using the light meter in an area of even lighting. Daylight is probably best, because indoor lighting in the home tends to have areas of bright light surrounded by much darker areas. Take light readings of objects that have differences in lightness and darkness because of their color and surface quality. Select one shutter speed for all of the readings and keep a record of the different f-stops needed to photograph the different objects. Before you take a reading, try to determine what the differences will be in terms of f-stops. Keep a record of your progress. List the object, your guess of the correct f-stop, and the f-stop needed according to the light meter. Practice until your guesses are reasonably close to the readings given by the light meter.

4. Find a dimly lit object (indoors would be best). Take a light meter reading of the object keeping the f-stop at f/11. What shutter speed would be necessary? Now, open the lens by one stop to f/8. What happens to the shutter speed? Explain.

F-Stop/Shutter Speed Relationship

Why does a camera have two different devices for controlling exposure? Sometimes enough light cannot be obtained with either the f-stop or the shutter alone. For example, if you are shooting with a hand-held camera with a fixed lens opening at a shutter speed of 1/60, you may not be able to let in enough light for a proper exposure. But you can enlarge an adjustable lens opening to increase the amount of light that will strike the film and increase the picture-taking range of the camera.

The same reasoning applies to situations in which there is too much light for a proper exposure. When you are able to adjust the camera lens to a very small opening and a fast shutter speed, you can reduce the amount of light much more than with a fixed lens opening. Your chances of getting a proper exposure in bright light are increased.

We have used an example here of a fixed and an adjustable lens opening. An adjustable lens opening and a fixed shutter speed would be as limiting as an adjustable shutter speed and a fixed lens opening.

Shutter speeds and lens openings (f-stop) always work together to determine exposure, and exposure must always be expressed in terms of *both* shutter speed and f-stop.

Assume that the following shutter speed/f-stop correlation is correct:

1000	500	250	125	60	30
f/2.8	f/4	f/5.6	f/8	f/11	f/16

A relatively slow shutter speed (1/15 sec) was used for this subject.

If you are taking a picture of a person running very fast and want to "freeze" the action, a very fast shutter speed is needed. Because a fast shutter speed "stops" the motion of the runner, the selection of 1/1000 at f/2.8 is a good choice. However, if you want to capture the motion of the runner by letting the image of the runner become slightly blurred, select a slow shutter speed. Because he moves across the picture plane while the shutter is open, the image is blurred. The selection of 1/30 at f/16 would be good. *Both combinations let the same amount of light reach the film; each is a proper exposure.* However, each combination produces a different picture. Your choice depends upon what effect you, as the photographer, want to communicate to the viewer.

Depth of Field. A second variable in the shutter speed/f-stop relationship deals with changes in the picture caused by the use of different f-stops. "Depth of field" is the amount of space that is in

33

1 *shallow depth of field at f/2.8*

2 *deeper depth of field at f/11*

focus both in front of and behind the exact point at which the camera lens is focused. *The larger the lens opening, the smaller the depth of field. The smaller the lens opening, the larger the depth of field.*

In photograph 1 (1/1000 at 2.8), only a single object is in sharp focus because a lens opening of f/2.8 gives a very small depth of field. Compare this with photograph 2 (1/60 at f/11) to see how much more space is in sharp focus because the lens has been "stopped down" four f-stops. Backing away from the subject will also increase the depth of field. *When depth of field is more important than movement, choose an exposure that gives more consideration to f-stop than to shutter speed.* These examples of photographs (chess board) illustrating the f-stop/depth of field relationship show that the photographer can control the camera so that it will produce a picture of the same situation in different ways.

Two other factors also affect depth of field: distance and focal length. The closer you are to the subject on which you are focusing, the smaller the depth of field. More depth of field is achieved the farther out the lens is focused. Compare the background area of the two photographs.

Focal length can be broadly defined as the distance between the optical center of the lens, when it is focused at infinity, and the focal point—the point where the image is in focus in the camera. The film is placed in the camera at the focal point, in the area known as the focal plane.

wide angle

normal

telephoto

You will recall that you could create wide-angle and telephoto effects with the pinhole camera by varying the pinhole-to-paper distance. When that distance was shorter than the diagonal measurement of the paper, the result was a wide-angle effect. Wide-angle lenses are made for most cameras. They are a short focal-length lens because the distance between the lens and the film is shorter than the film's diagonal measurement. Conversely, when the distance between the lens and the film is longer than the film's diagonal measurement, the result is a telephoto effect. The telephoto, then, is a long focal-length lens.

Depth of field is greatest with a short focal-length lens (wide angle). In other words, the shorter the focal length, the greater the depth of field. Compare the three photographs on the preceding page. All were taken in the same light and with the same shutter speed (1/250) at f/16. The first photograph was taken with a short focal-length lens—notice that both the background and the foreground are in focus, indicating a greater depth of field. The second picture was shot with a normal focal-length lens, probably the same length as the one in your camera. Here, though, the background fades out of focus. A long focal-length lens (telephoto) was used in the third photo. Only the subject is in focus—the background directly behind the subject is completely out of focus.

To summarize, three factors determine depth of field: (1) f-stop (also called aperture or lens opening); (2) focus; and (3) focal length. The smaller the aperture, the greater the depth of field. The

Three factors that determine depth of field.

1 *f/stop*

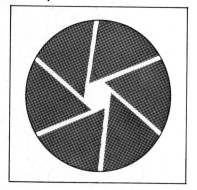

2 *subject-to-camera distance*

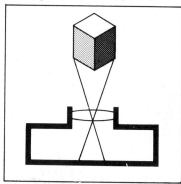

3 *focal length of lens*

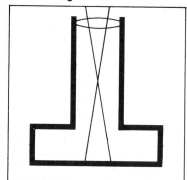

further the distance between the lens and the subject, the greater the depth of field. And finally, the shorter the focal length, the greater the depth of field.

(Chapter 10 will introduce more technical information about lenses.)

Assignment: Depth of Field

1. Place three similar objects (for instance, matching chairs) 4 feet from each other in a row—outdoors if possible. Otherwise, try shooting indoors in a brightly lit room. Stand 8 feet from the closest chair and focus on the middle chair. Take a light meter reading and expose so that you are shooting at f/4. Then adjust your shutter so that you are shooting at f/8. Adjust your shutter again so that you are exposing at f/16. What effect do you think each different f-stop will have on the photograph? Explain.
2. Photograph a person standing next to a fence. Stand 10 feet away from the person and focus on his or her face, making sure you are at an angle to the fence. Take a light meter reading so that you are exposing at f/2.8. What will be the effect? What would you have to do if you wanted the whole fence in focus? Why?
3. Photograph a moving car at 1/30. What will be the effect? Photograph another moving car so that you are using 1/500 instead. What will be the visual difference between the two photographs?

Pat Thomas

Basic Film Development 4

After you have taken a picture, curiosity alone will make you want to see it, even if you suspect it is overexposed or underexposed or out of focus. Developing the film is the halfway point between taking the picture and printing the negative. It makes visible and permanent the latent image that is recorded on the emulsion of the film. Film development is a chemical process, involving a very definite series of steps. If the exposure was correct, this procedure, followed carefully, will produce a good quality negative. That negative, in turn, will determine the quality of the resulting print.

Almost all films are sensitive to every color of light, and so film developing must be done in total darkness. Ironically, the same light needed to take the picture will ruin it when the film is unloaded from its light-tight packaging.

There are two methods of film development, one using open trays of chemicals, the other, a closed tank. The tank method is the more efficient and does not require total darkness after the film is loaded into the developing tank. It gives you a better chance of getting a good quality negative. The tray method is seldom used for developing roll film because all the steps must be carried out in complete darkness. However, it is useful when developing cut film (sheet film).

The Tank Method

The basic developing tank consists of: the tank itself, the lid (to make it light-tight), and the reel (to hold the film). Tanks are made of either plastic or stainless steel; many different brands are available.

Plastic developing tanks usually are cheaper than stainless steel. Most of them have reels that adjust to accommodate film sizes from 35mm up to 120. To load the plastic tank, (See Fig. 4-1) first adjust the reel to the size of the film. For Instamatic-type cartridges or 35mm, the flange of the adjustable reel is to be moved down as far as it will go. For 127 film, the reel is locked into the

Fig. 4-1
plastic adjustable reel

open cartridge

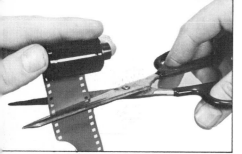

cut off tapered film leader

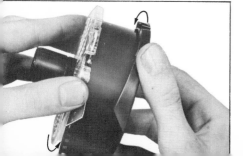

remove tape

insert film through slots

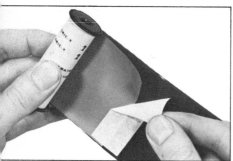

rotate sides in counter directions

second notch. When using 120 or 620 film, spread the reel out as far as possible until it locks into position.

The next steps must be carried out in total darkness. Make sure the reel is clean and dry before attempting to load the film into it. To load 35mm, first remove the cartridge that encloses the film, using a bottle opener to remove the flat flange on the top of the cartridge. Do it with care. Take the spool of film from the cartridge, but leave the film on the spool. (Keep the film perpendicular rather than letting it swing back and forth like a pendulum.) With a scissors, cut off the tapered beginning of the film (the leader).

With roll films (sizes 828, 127, 620, 120), you need only break the seal to load it. The film curls as it is separated from the paper backing, and it should be handled only by the edges to prevent fingerprints on the emulsion. The film is attached to the paper with tape, which must be removed before the film is loaded into the reel. Otherwise it will prevent proper loading.

If 126 film (Instamatic-type) is used, remove the film by gripping the cartridge with both hands and twisting it until it breaks in half. The film is in the larger of the two chambers. After that chamber is broken too, separate the film from the paper backing in the same manner as roll film.

After the film has been removed from its container, insert three or four inches of the film into the reel by pushing it carefully through the entrance slots (the thickest part of the flanges). As you do this, follow the natural curl of the film so that the emulsion side will face toward the core of the reel and be less likely to be scratched and will be easier to load. Take hold of the edges of the reel. With the Anscomatic tank, hold the clear flange (the movable section) in the left hand, the black flange in the right hand. Twist the black flange forward (away from you) as far as it will go; then twist it back (toward you) as far as it will go. Continue this procedure until the film is wound on the reel. If you are loading 35mm film, this action will stop when the spool reaches the entrance. Cut the film at the edge of the spool and continue winding it onto the reel. If you are using the G.A.F. tank, you will hear two slight clicks when all the film passes the entrance slots. You can make sure that all the film is wound on the reel by running your finger around the entrance slots. The edge of the film should be past the entrance.

If the film does not go on the reel smoothly, do not force it, or you may mar the film permanently. Do not try to pull the film back through the film entrance. Instead, pull off the adjustable flange, remove the film, readjust the reel to the film size, and start again. After all the film is on the reel, place it in the tank, keeping the clear flange on top. Put the lid on the tank by turning it clockwise. The room light may now be turned on since the tank is light-tight.

The Stainless Steel Tank

Loading the stainless steel reel and tank is slightly more difficult, and so it is suggested that you practice loading in daylight before attempting the real thing. Like plastic tanks, stainless steel tanks are made by different manufacturers and so many differ slightly. To be sure you load the reel properly, read the instruction manual and check with your teacher. The instructions given here cover loading a typical stainless steel reel. The photographs on the right illustrate three important steps in loading such a reel.

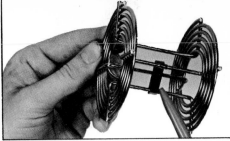

stainless steel reel

Remove the film from its protective container as described earlier. Hold the reel in your left hand so that the opening of the retaining device on the core points upward. Hold the beginning of the film, following the natural curvature between your thumb and forefinger, and curving it slightly so that the film vaults out a bit. Don't curve the film too much or the film will buckle. Lift the retaining device on the reel with your left thumb and let the film enter the slot until it stops. Use a little pressure on the retaining device, which will spike through the film, locking it to the reel. Having done this, hold the reel with one hand and turn it slowly counterclockwise, using the thumb and forefinger of the other hand to curve and guide the film along the edge of the reel.

retaining device holds film

After all the film is wound onto the reel, check to make sure that it is loaded correctly. Simply feel the top and bottom of the reel—if no film is projecting above the spirals, you're ready. If the film is projecting through, then start over again. When the film is loaded properly, close the top end of the tank and turn on the lights. Some manufacturers make automatic loading devices for their reels. These devices automatically curve the film for you.

curve and guide film as reel is rotated

One advantage of the stainless steel tank is that you usually buy the reels and tank separately. This allows you to buy a tank big enough to hold one, two, three, four, or even eight rolls of film at the same time. Another advantage of stainless steel is that the tank can hold different sizes of reels, letting you develop several sizes of film at the same time.

Developing the Film

The Chemicals. The chemicals needed to develop the latent image on film are the same as those used to bring out the latent images in pinhole photographs and photograms. Again, they are (1) the developer, (2) the stop bath, and (3) the fixer.

The job of the developer is to convert the silver halides (which make up the latent image on the exposed emulsion) to blackened particles of silver that clump together during development to form a visible photographic image. Because the job of the developer is so complex, it contains a mixture of several chemicals. Chemical formulas of the developers on the market today vary. However, most of them contain (1) a solvent, (2) a reducer, (3) an activator, (4) a preservative, and (5) a restrainer. In most, the solvent is water, because in order to work, the other chemicals must be in solution. The reducer causes the actual chemical breakdown of the exposed silver salts. The activator in the developer does two things. First, it renders the developing solution alkaline rather than acid; and second, it helps the water to soften the gelatin of the film so that the reducer can separate the exposed silver salts. The preservative agent in a developer reduces or retards the oxidizing (combining with air) of the reducers. Without it, reducing agents will deposit rust-colored stains on the film. The job of the restrainer is to control the action of the developing agents, which could attack the unexposed as well as the exposed silver grains, causing a chemical fog on the film.

One last note about developers: Film manufacturers usually tell you on the film information sheet which developers work best for their films. It is best to trust their judgment and not experiment too much with unknown developers. Some developers are made specifically for films, while others are made to be used with photo papers. Ignoring this difference will result in a poor negative or a poor print.

The next chemical used in the developing process—the stop bath—stops the action of the developer. Some stop bath solutions (such as Kodak's Indicator stop bath) contain a chemical indicator that lets you know they are no longer working effectively. When the stop bath is yellow, it's okay. When the indicator turns the bath a purple color, then it is time to use a new mixture. A stop bath has one other function—to preserve the life of the next chemical, the fixer. The fixer removes the unexposed silver deposits, thereby eliminating the sensitivity of the film to light. The fixer also contains a hardener which makes the emulsion of the film harder and less likely to be scratched.

These are the basic chemicals used in developing film. Two other chemicals are also often used in this process. The hypo eliminater is a solution that neutralizes the fixer, greatly reducing the time that negatives must be washed. Unless the negatives are washed thoroughly, the hypo that remains on them will continue to affect the emulsion and will bleach out your negatives. After the wash, a wetting agent can be employed. To explain this simply, a wetting agent makes the water "wetter" so that the film will dry without water marks and streaks.

The Developing Process. Once the film is loaded on the reel and in the tank, you are ready to start developing it. In addition to the chemicals, you should have a thermometer, a photographic sponge and two film clips. The thermometer should be an accurate one. Don't trust the ones that come with plastic tanks—they are usually

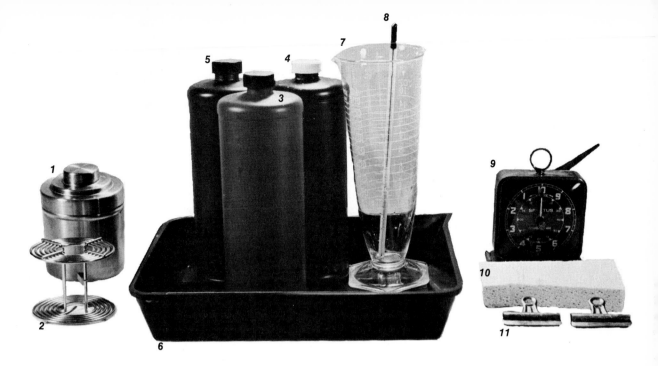

off by as much as six degrees. *You must check the temperature of all the chemical solutions, especially the developer.* The developer should be at about 68°F., although anywhere between 65° to 75° is usable. The length of time the developer remains in the tank depends on the type of film being developed and on the temperature of the developer. By referring to the information sheet that is packed with the film, you'll learn how long the developer should be left in the tank. (Another good source for information is the Kodak® publication, *Master Darkroom Dataguide.* This book describes all development times with most black and white Kodak® films (except graphic arts, x-ray and other special-purpose films) at all usable temperatures.

The temperatures of the other chemicals, including the wash water, should be near that of the developer. If the film is subjected to drastic changes in temperatures, large grains which will form a textured image in the negative. In some cases, temperature changes can cause reticulation—the physical cracking or wrinkling of the emulsion. After you have checked the temperatures and timing for the developer, pour it into the tank through the opening in the lid. Do not remove the tank lid to pour in the chemical. In a stainless tank, there is a second lid over a little spout, this lid is removed to add the developer. In a plastic tank, just pour the chemical through the hole in the top of the tank.

It is important to agitate the film while it is in each of the chemical solutions. This step is particularly critical when the developer solution is in the tank. If you are using a stainless steel tank, turn

Preparing to process

1 *stainless steel tank*
2 *stainless steel reel*
3 *developer (mixed)*
4 *stop bath*
5 *hypo (mixed)*
6 *water jacket*
7 *measuring beaker*
8 *thermometer*
9 *clock (with second hand)*
10 *sponge*
11 *clips*

Each processing step is labeled with the chemical, temperature, and activity required during that step. Follow manufacturer's instructions for the specific time each step requires.

the tank gently over and back two or three times during a 5-second period once every 30 seconds. However, during the first 30 seconds be sure that the developer is in the tank, agitate the film more vigorously and rap the tank sharply against the sink or counter several times. This 30-second initial agitation and the rapping of the tank will release any air bubbles in the developing solution. Air bubbles can adhere to the emulsion, causing tiny clear spots on the negative that will appear as black spots in the print.

In plastic tanks (such as the G.A.F.), agitate the film by rotating the thermometer rod that comes with the tank. After the developer is poured into the tank, insert the rod into the hole and turn it back and forth briskly five or six times. Without tilting the tank, rap it sharply against the surface to dislodge the air bubbles. From then on agitate the film for 5 seconds every 30 seconds by *gently* turning the rod back and forth.

Agitating the film too much may cause streaks to appear on the negative. When using the agitator rod of a plastic tank; be careful not to spin the rod like a screwdriver, as this will make the negatives overdeveloped and uneven.

When this step is finished, pour out the developer and pour in the stop bath quickly. Be sure that all tanks are filled to capacity with each chemical solution being used. (You want all of each

load reel and place inside tank

developer
68°
pour into tank

agitate as indicated

pour out developer

stop bath
68°
pour in/agitate

pour out stop bath

hypo
68°
pour in/agitate

pour out hypo

hypo eliminator
68°
pour in/agitate

negative to be developed, not just the bottom half.) The stop bath remains in the tank for no longer than 45 seconds in a small developing tank. Agitate the tank once during this immersion. Be sure that the stop bath is within the 65° to 75° temperature range.

Now pour the stop bath out and the hypo fixer in. Check the hypo before pouring it in to make sure it is within the right temperature range. Agitate the film periodically so that the hypo will reach all the film. How long the hypo should remain in the tank depends on the brand being used. After that time is up, pour the hypo out and open the lid. Rinse the film on the reel for 30 seconds. Pour the hypo neutralizer in for the period of time recommended by the maker. After the neutralizer is removed, you are ready for the final rinse. The temperature of the water also should be within the 65° to 75° range. Wash for approximately 20 minutes with rapid changes of water. Empty the tank periodically to make sure that fresh water is entering the tank.

Now remove the film gently from the reel. Be sure to remember that the emulsion is soft and can be scratched easily. Attach a film clip to each end of the film and, holding the film by the clips, suspend it in a narrow loop so that the looped portion is completely immersed in the tank. Then raise and lower the film to run the loop portion through the solution quickly. After three or four passes through the wetting agent, hang the film to dry in a dust-free place. Wipe the wet film gently with a photographic sponge to remove the excess water. The purpose of these last two steps is to ensure a clean negative, free from dust, dirt, or lint

pour out hypo eliminator

water
68°
wash film

that otherwise may stick to the film permanently. It will also cut drying time and prevent water spots from forming on the negative.

The Tray Method

The tray method of developing film works best for sheet film (cut film) and should be used for roll film only in an emergency.

Arrange three trays, large enough to handle the size of film being developed, on a table. The first tray is for the developer, the second for the stop bath, and the third for the hypo fixer. Pour about 1½ inches of chemical solution into each of the trays. Take the temperature of the developer to determine the length of time the film is to be immersed. After this is known, test the other two chemicals to make sure they are within the usable temperature range of 65° to 75°. From this point on, work in total darkness. Now immerse the film in the first tray, containing the developer. If you are using sheet film, be sure that the notched edge of the film is to the right facing the top edge of the tray.

Agitate the tray constantly, but not rapidly. Just rock it back and forth a few times. The film will move from one side of the tray to the other while developing. Keep your hands out of the developer until you are ready to immerse the film in the stop bath. The film stays in the stop bath for 30 seconds. After this time is up, move it to the fixer. Handle the film very carefully, touching only the

sponge film down gently

Each processing step is labeled with the chemical, temperature, and activity required during that step. Follow manufacturer's instructions for the specific time each step requires.

developer
68°
agitate

stop bath
68°
agitate

hypo
68°
agitate

edges, since it is very soft and can scratch very easily. After the film has been in the fixer for one minute, room light may be turned on to view the negative. The film should remain in the hypo for the prescribed time, after which it should be handled as in the final steps of the tank method.

Care of Negatives

Negatives are delicate. They can be wrinkled and scratched very easily. Scratches on a negative will appear as black or white marks on the final print. To avoid scratches, it is best to handle the film only by the edges. After the film is dry, roll film should be cut into strips about six inches long. Never cut it into individual negatives, since they are too hard to handle. These cut strips should be stored in negative envelopes, which are available at any camera shop. Keep your negatives in a clean, dry place.

Problems in Development

If all the steps in the process of development are followed precisely, and if your film was exposed correctly, the result should be a high quality negative that can become a high quality print. However, mistakes can happen. These photographs illustrate some common mistakes in developing and how they will affect the final negative

inspect negative

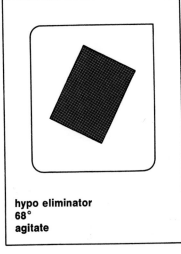

hypo eliminator
68°
agitate

water
68°
wash film

overdeveloped

underdeveloped and carelessly handled

Development time differs with the type of film being used, the type of developer, and the temperature of that developer. In the first set of photos, notice how light the negative is. The resulting print is too dark. In the second set, the negative was developed at the proper temperature (68°) for the time that the manufacturer recommended for that type of film. This negative has a good level of contrast and is neither underdeveloped (too light) or overdeveloped (too dark). The third set was purposely overdeveloped, and the result is a negative that is too contrasting and dense. Thus, the print lacks detail.

These examples of underdevelopment, normal development, and overdevelopment illustrate what can happen to a properly exposed negative. However, you may want to over- or underdevelop a negative intentionally. If, for example, you overexposed the negative when taking the picture, you may want to underdevelop it. Underdeveloping an overexposed negative will lighten it and compensate for its density. On the other hand, suppose that you know your negative is underexposed. By overdeveloping it, you'll add density to the negative and darken it.

The purpose of agitation in the developing process is to move the solution inside the tank so that a steady supply of fresh developer reaches the emulsion of the film throughout the developing period. If the tank (or tray) is not agitated enough, the negative will be underdeveloped. But if there is too much agitation, then overdevelopment will occur, especially at the edges of the film. In the center set, the right amount of agitation was used.

Certain ingredients in the fixer make the timing of the film's immersion important. If the negative is immersed in the fixer for too short a period, unexposed silver will remain on it and the neg-

fogged film

overagitated

ative will be too opaque to be printed, as in the first set of photos. The second set of photos shows a negative that was left in the fixer for the proper length of time. In the event that the negative remains in the fixer too long, then the fixer begins to attack not only the unexposed portions of the negative, but also the parts that were exposed.

If the negative is not washed and dried properly, two things may go wrong. First, the negative may start to turn yellow and fade because some of the fixer is still acting on it. Second, the negative may have spots on it. Wash and dry your negative carefully and thoroughly. There are no shortcuts in film development.

Assignment: Basic Film Development

1. The temperature of the chemicals used to develop the latent image in film should remain constant from the developer through the wash. What do you think will happen to the emulsion if temperatures vary greatly from one chemical to the next? Explain your reasons.
2. It is important to agitate the film while it is in each chemical. Why? What could happen to the negatives if they are not agitated? What could happen if they are agitated too much?
3. Can overdevelopment cause overexposure? Can underdevelopment cause underexposure? Is it possible to correct overexposure with underdevelopment? If so, is it possible to correct underexposure with overdevelopment? Explain.
4. Assuming that your negatives were developed, washed, and stored correctly, is it possible that they can fade over a period of time? If so, explain your reasons.

Basic Printmaking:
The contact print

5

Making a contact print from a negative allows the photographer to see the picture in its correct tonal range. You have already made a kind of contact print when you made positive images from your photogram negatives. Here the only difference is that the developed film, not a paper negative, is placed in contact with the paper.

Photographically speaking, a contact print is a negative of the negative. But this new "negative" is made on photographic paper and has the same areas of light and dark as the subject matter you originally photographed. In terms of your subject, it is a "positive." The image on the paper will be the same size as the negative. Because the image is small, the contact print is useful only to help the photographer choose which negatives to enlarge.

The contact printing process begins with the passage of light through the negative onto photo paper. The negative and paper are placed in a tight contact with each other, emulsion to emulsion. In other words, the dull side of the negative is placed in contact with the shiny side of the paper. Contact printing a negative involves the same six steps as photogram printing: (1) exposure, (2) developer, (3) stop bath, (4) fixer, (5) washing, and (6) drying. It is done under safelight illumination in a photo darkroom.

The first step is to lay the negatives on the paper; emulsion sides together. There are three simple devices that can be used to hold the paper and negatives tightly together. (See Fig. 5-1.) The simplest device is a piece of plate glass, clean and unscratched, large enough to cover the entire sheet of paper (11" x 14" works well). The paper is placed on a table or counter, the emulsion side facing up. The emulsion (dull) side of the negative is then placed on the paper. The glass is placed on top, holding the two together tightly. If you wish, you can lay several negatives down on a larger sheet of photographic paper (say, 8" x 10"). This allows you to see at one time all the negatives from a roll of film. You can then compare and choose which negatives are correctly exposed, in focus, and composed to show the image you want. (See Fig. 5-2.) The contact print made in this way is called a proof sheet.

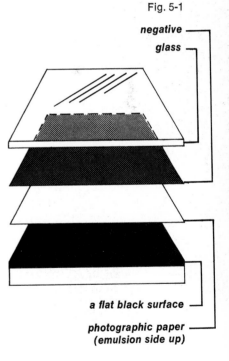

Fig. 5-1

negative ——

glass ——

a flat black surface ——

photographic paper ——
(emulsion side up)

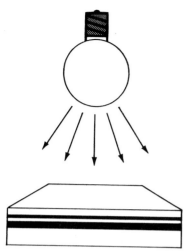

press glass, negative, paper, and board together firmly before exposing

Another device is the contact printing frame, a wooden or metal frame with a spring back. The spring back holds the negative and paper together. Again, the emulsion sides face each other in the frame.

Neither of these devices contains a light source for exposure. Thus, a white light is needed. Generally, a bare light bulb can be used if it is about 3 feet directly above the paper.

The third device, the contact printer, has its own light source. Because the light source is so close to the paper, you must use a specially designed photo paper, which is less sensitive to light than others. It is called simply "contact printing paper." To use a contact printer, first place the negative on the glass so that the emulsion side (dull side) faces up. Next, lay the paper on the negative so that the emulsion side faces down. The lid of the printer keeps the two in contact.

Exposure time varies with the type of paper being used, the type of light, and the negatives themselves. The darker the negative, the more time it takes for light to penetrate it and expose the paper. Generally, exposure will range from 1 to 5 seconds. (The light from a photo enlarger can also be used for contact printing. To learn how to use the enlarger for this purpose, refer to the enlarger section in Chapter 6.) Keep in mind that the exposure on a contact sheet is an average, and that pictures that appear too light or too dark on the contact sheet can be printed at their proper density (darkness or lightness) when they are printed individually.

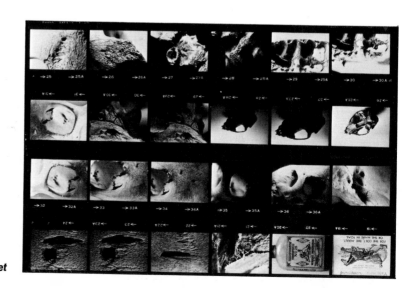

Fig. 5-2
contact sheet

Processing the Print

Print development follows the same basic process as film development. It uses a developer, a stop bath, and a fixer. However, the method of handling the print is different, as well as the time that the paper is immersed in the various chemical solutions.

Three trays are set up in a row. These trays should be a little larger than the paper being developed, since it is important that the entire print be immersed in the chemical solution at the same time.

The first tray is filled with developer solution, the second with stop bath, and the third with hypo fixer. It is advisable to use print tongs rather than your hands when moving the print from one tray filled with solution to the next. This also will help prevent you from getting a skin rash or irritation from the chemicals.

Another important reason for keeping your hands out of the chemicals is that you must not contaminate the solutions, especially the developer. While the print itself will contaminate the stop bath with developer, the fixer with stop bath, it will not ruin those chemicals. However, if stop bath or fixer gets into the developer, its capacity or ability to develop prints will be reduced. Worse yet, contaminated hands can cause finger prints and stains on photo paper, thus ruining it.

Because the image on an exposed sheet of paper is latent, a developer must be used to make it visible. Certain developers are designed to be used with photographic paper rather than with film.

1 *sponge*
2 *developer*
3 *stop bath*
4 *hypo*
5 *measuring cup*
6 *clock*
7 *tongs*
8 *4 trays*
9 *window wiper*
10 *safelight*
11 *book blotter (dryer)*

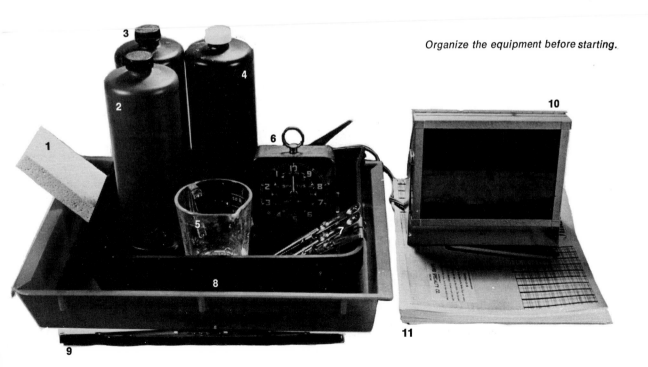

Organize the equipment before starting.

53

There are many brands available, such as Kodak's Dektol® and Ektaplo®, as well as Ethols LPD.®

After the exposure, immediately slip the paper into the developer tray noting the time. The paper may be placed in the tray either face down or face up for the first few seconds, but should be turned face up as soon as it is thoroughly wet. The important thing is to get the entire print into the tray quickly. Don't let one end of the sheet hang over the tray while the rest is in the developer. Also, until the paper has been completely saturated, be careful to keep the corners of the print in the developer, as they may tend to curl upward and develop unevenly. Once the print is in the solution, rock the tray gently back and forth. This agitation should not be violent or fast; its purpose is only to keep the solution constantly moving across the emulsion on the paper. Use print tongs occasionally to poke down the corners of the paper. If you do not use tongs, then try not to touch the surface of the print unnecessarily. Also avoid continued pressure on one area of the print, because the heat of your body will warm the developer and make it work faster, causing a dark spot in that area.

The image on the paper will begin to appear in about 30 seconds if your print has been properly exposed. Even if the print looks too dark after a minute in the developer, do not remove it from the solution. The print must remain in the developer for 1½ to 2 minutes. However, do not leave it longer than 2 minutes, or it will probably develop brown stains.

Each processing step is labeled with the chemical, recommended time in the chemical, and the action required during the recommended time. Gray background indicates safelight illumination.

developer
3 seconds
immerse print

developer
1 ½ minute
agitate

stop bath
30 seconds
agitate

If you remove the print from the developer too soon because it appears to be getting too dark; the result will be a muddy, gray image lacking contrast. There will be no sharp blacks or whites in the print. One way to correct a print that is too dark after 1½ minutes in the developer is to shorten the exposure time. You can also close the lens down on the enlarger. If the print is completely black, then cut the exposure time in half and try again. If the print remains in the developer for 2 minutes and is very pale or completely white, then double the exposure time. Always remember this important technique: *Lightness or darkness of a print is controlled by the exposure time and should not be manipulated by varying the time in the developer.*

After the print has been in the developer for at least 1½ minutes and no longer than 2 minutes, hold it by one corner to drain for a few moments and then place it in the stop bath. Agitate the print in the stop bath for about 30 seconds. During this period you may hear a whistling sound coming from the solution—this indicates that the sodium carbonate from the developer is being broken down to carbon dioxide which is being released as a gas. Do not leave the print in the stop bath longer than one minute, as it may start to stain out the image. After 30 seconds in the stop bath, drain the print as before and then immerse it in the hypo fixer.

If the whistling sound continues after the print is in the hypo, it may indicate that the stop bath is weakened and should be replaced. It may also indicate that the print wasn't in the stop bath

Illumination used to inspect print should be similar to illumination used to view displayed print.

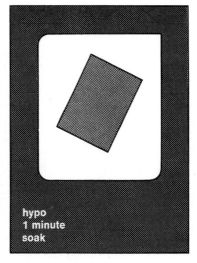

hypo
1 minute
agitate

hypo
1 minute
soak

inspection

long enough or that you did not drain the print enough when changing from tray to tray.

Once the print is in the hypo, agitate it for about a minute and then let it soak in the solution for another minute before inspecting it with room light. If other prints are in the same hypo tray, then agitate them every few minutes. The print should remain in the hypo for the time recommended by the manufacturer. Generally, this is about 8 minutes. If the print remains in the hypo for too long, more than 10 minutes, the image may absorb hypo in such a way as to resist washing. Eventually the hypo will stain the print. If the print is exposed to white light immediately after immersion in the fixer, it will "fog." But if the print fogs under white light after two minutes in the hypo, then the hypo should be replaced as it is no longer working.

To examine the print, it is best to place it in a clean tray and take it out of the darkroom. Otherwise the room light may ruin somebody else's photo paper. The tray will prevent the hypo from dripping off the print. Dried fixer is difficult to remove from floors, cabinets, and the like.

After the print has been in the fixer for the recommended time, begin the wash cycle. Although it is not a necessity, hypo eliminator removes most of the hypo fixer, thereby shortening the washing time. When using this method, wash the prints in a tray with running water for two minutes. After this time, soak the prints in the hypo eliminator for the manufacturer's recommended time, rocking the tray.

hypo
6 minutes
agitate

hypo eliminator
see instructions
agitate

water
20 minutes
wash

Once the prints leave the hypo eliminator solution, they should be washed again in running water for about 15 to 20 minutes after the last print is placed in the wash tray. If no hypo cleaning agent was used, then they should be washed for at least one hour. Use a large tray for washing, as the water must flow freely between the prints. It is best to wash only a few prints at a time to keep the prints from bunching up. If an unwashed print is put into a full tray of washed prints, it will contaminate them, and all of them will have to be rewashed. If a print is not washed sufficiently, it will turn yellowish or fade over a period of years.

Next the washed print must be dried. There are several ways to do this, depending on the equipment available. The easiest method is to use a photo blotter roll or book. First, squeeze off the excess water by placing the print on a sheet of glass and using a photo squeegee, a cellulose sponge, or even a clean window-wiper blade. Before doing this, place a tray underneath the glass to catch the excess water. If you are using a roll, place the prints on it and roll it up again, using a rubber band to hold it. If you use a blotter book, place some heavy books on top of it to keep the prints compressed. Leave the prints in the blotters for a couple of days to let them dry completely.

For quicker drying, an electric dryer can be used. At least two types of dryers are available, the rotary (drum) and the flat bed. (double sided). The drum dryer should be turned on at least ten minutes before use and allowed to reach an operating temperature of about 275°F. After squeezing the water from the washed print,

wipe down

place it on the dryer blanket face down. By turning the handle, the moving belt will carry the print around the drum. Leave it in the dryer for approximately 10 minutes. Some dryers of this type are called continuous belt; the turning of the handle is unnecessary, since the dryer drum will rotate automatically.

To use the flat-bed dryer, set the thermostat on the dryer to "medium." Squeeze off the excess water and place the print on the bed of the dryer facing up. Pull the canvas over the print and lock it closed. After five minutes, raise the thermostat temperature to "high" for another five minutes. Then remove the print from the dryer.

It is important to dry only thoroughly washed prints in an electric dryer. If the print still contains some hypo, it will contaminate the blanket or canvas of the dryer. This will in turn contaminate clean prints that touch it.

One type of paper available can simply be air dried without curling. RC paper has a resin-coated base which, when just wiped down with a photo sponge will dry in a matter of minutes. However, RC paper should never be dried in an electric dryer, as the heat will cause the coating of the paper to melt on the dryer. Not only will this ruin the print, but it may also ruin the dryer.

A Word about Papers

As you know, prints are made by light passing through the negative onto light-sensitive paper—photographic paper. The tones in the negative are the opposite of those in the original subject— black areas on the negative were light in the original scene, light areas on the negative were originally dark. Thus, the print reverses the negative image to a positive.

Photographic paper is similar to film except that the film emulsion is on an acetate base while the paper emulsion is on the paper itself. Another difference is that most photo paper is insensitive to red or yellow light and so can be handled under those colors of light (the darkroom safelight). Most films are sensitive to all colors and so are developed in total darkness.

Photo paper is usually classified according to five qualities: (1) tone, (2) surface, (3) speed, (4) weight, and (5) contrast.

Some photo papers have a "warm" tone while others are "cold." Warm papers yield a brownish black, while a cold-tone paper yields a blue black. Warm-tone papers are used primarily for portraits of people; cold-tone papers are used for most other types of photographs (cool black usually looks "blacker" than warm black).

All photographic papers are made with different surface finishes. Some surfaces are a dull matte, while others resemble silk or burlap. Some papers are ultra glossy; others have a lustre finish.

The speed of the paper (its sensitivity to light) varies with each manufacturer and each type of paper. Basically, though, there are two general classifications: contact printing paper and enlarging paper. Contact paper is slower in speed than enlarging paper and is used in making contact prints.

Photographic paper is available in three thicknesses or weights: single, medium, and double. As their names imply, double-weight paper is about twice as thick as single weight, while medium weight falls between them.

Contrast in papers plays an important part in printmaking. For instance, if your negative was underexposed (too light), contrast can be added in the print by using a higher contrast paper. If the negative was overexposed (too dark), then it also has too much contrast. In this case, you would use a paper that is low in contrast.

There are two methods in making prints: contact printing and enlarging. In this chapter we have discussed making a contact print, one that is the same size as the negative. In the next chapter, we will discuss the methods for enlarging photographs.

Assignment: Contact Printing

1. In contact printing, it is important that the emulsion of the negative is placed in contact with the emulsion of the paper. What would happen if the nonemulsion side of the negative were placed in contact with the paper?
2. Is it possible to make a large (11″ x 14″) contact print?
3. Suppose you have three negatives: one is overexposed; one is underexposed; and one is correct. Which would require the longest exposure in contact printing? The shortest? Explain.
4. Why are you able to use a safelight when developing contact prints and are not able to when developing film?

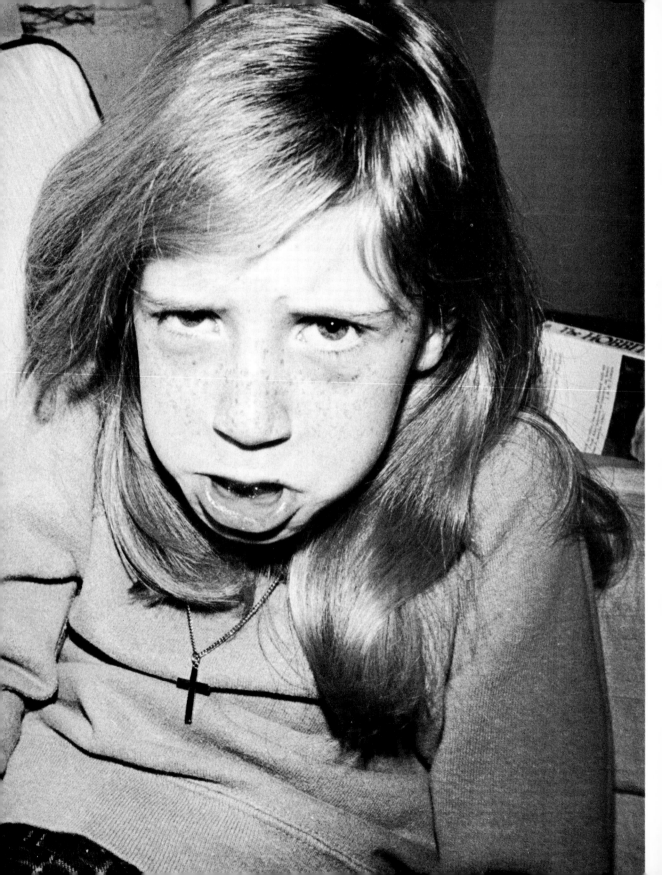

Basic Enlarging

6

In painting, the finished product is displayed, not the preliminary sketches. In silk screen printmaking, the prints are framed and viewed, not the screens used to make them. So it is true in photographic printmaking, that is, it is not the negative that is viewed, but the print.

The photographic printmaker interprets each negative. He or she can influence the final result by understanding and using technical manipulations to raise the quality of the photograph to an artistic level. The printmaker can correct for shortcomings in the negatives —emphasizing a composition by eliminating part of the image, subduing unwanted light areas, or making areas lighter. In the safelight illumination of a darkroom, the photographer makes the print that will communicate to the viewer the essence of the idea recorded on the film.

For many photographers, enlarging the negative is the climax of the creative process that began when they first decided to take the picture. The first contact print of the negative transforms that image into a recognizable form. It can be a moment of complete triumph over the technical considerations of photography, or it can be a moment of discouragement. However, the contact print is small. Enlarging the negative can increase the beauty of the image—or may just magnify its deficiencies.

The physical processes of enlarging are essentially the same as those of contact printing. The enlarger is the printmaker's tool for transforming the negative image, through interpretation, to the positive image, the enlargement.

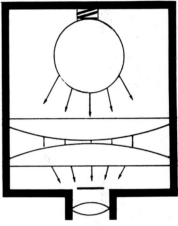

Condenser enlarger

Diffusion enlarger

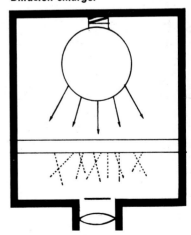

Condenser enlarger
Condenser lenses collect light and direct it coherently towards the negative and lens.

Diffusion enlarger
A frosted glass plate scatters the light falling on the negative, causing the enlarger lens to project a softer image.

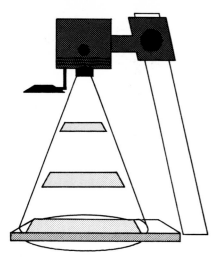

Fig. 6-1

Raise enlarger head to enlarge image.

The Enlarger

An enlarger is basically a camera in reverse. Rather than absorb light, it projects it. An enlarger contains a strong light source and some sort of optical system through which the light rays pass before they reach the negative. The rays are then focused on the photographic paper by a lens attached to the enlarger. An enlarging easel holds the paper in place.

The sole purpose of the enlarger is to increase the size of the negative image that is being projected. Thus, from a very small negative, prints can be made that measure 8″ x 10″ and even larger. The size of the projected image is controlled by the height of the enlarger above the paper. The greater the distance between the paper and the lens of the enlarger, the larger the magnification will be. The size of the projected image is changed by raising and lowering the entire body of the enlarger on the vertical column. (See Fig. 6-1.) Then the image must be brought into fine focus by turning the focusing knob on the enlarger. Focusing will again alter the size of the image somewhat, so it may be necessary to raise or lower the enlarger and then again focus the image.

All enlargers have lenses. The size of the lens (focal length) depends on the size of the negative being enlarged. Generally, the focal length of the lens on the enlarger will match the "normal" focal length on the camera for a particular size of film. For instance, the normal size focal length lens for a 35mm camera is 50mm. Thus, a 50mm lens is used on the enlarger. A normal lens for a 2¼″ x 2¼″ camera is 75-85 mm; this size of lens would also be used on the enlarger. If a 50mm lens were used to enlarge a 2¼″ x 2¼″ negative, it might not cover the full area of the negative but might cut off the corners of the image. On the other hand, if a 75mm lens were used to enlarge a 35mm negative, then it would produce a smaller magnification than a 50mm lens, assuming that the enlarger-to-paper distance is not changed.

The brightness of the image is controlled by the iris on the lens. The more the lens is "stopped down," the less light will pass through it. Brightness also decreases as the enlarger is raised to give greater magnification.

The photographic paper must be kept perfectly flat during the exposure, or else one area of the paper will be out of focus while the rest is in focus. Enlarging easels are designed to hold the photo paper completely flat during the exposure. Most easels are adjusted by moving the thin metal strips to form a mask; they can be masked off for various standard paper sizes, such as 3½″ x 5″, 5″ x 7″, 8″ x 10″, and 11″ x 14″. The printing paper is inserted from one end and slides along the guides of the easel until it is centered within the mask. The emulsion side of the paper faces up toward the enlarger lens.

A special enlarger timer can be used to control the amount of exposure. Most of the timers on the market have a range from

1 second to 60 seconds. Usually there is a manual light switch to turn the enlarger on for focusing. Once the timer has been set for the period of exposure, a button is pushed to begin the timing. The timer then automatically turns on the enlarger light and turns it off when the exposure has been completed. Although it is not as accurate, a switch on the enlarger line also can be used to turn the enlarger on and off to control the exposure. In this case, you must use a wristwatch to check the exposure time.

Making Contact Prints with the Enlarger

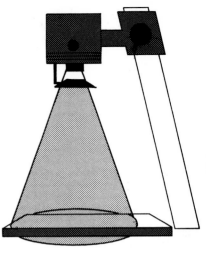

The enlarger can also be used as a convenient light source for making contact prints or proof sheets. To do this, set up the printing frame or the plate glass as you would for enlarging. Raise the enlarger so that the light covers the entire area of the paper. If the red filter is swung underneath the lens, you can turn the enlarger light on to make sure that the area is covered. (See Fig. 6-2.) This red filter acts like a safelight so that the light will not affect the paper. When you have checked the light area, turn the enlarger on with either the timer or the line switch. (The red filter should, of course, be swung back out of the way of the lens during the exposure.) Process this print in the same manner as described earlier.

Fig. 6-2
Use red filter to preview light coverage.

Making an Enlargement

Although enlargers vary in the way they work, the basic steps in enlarging are the same. Assume that you have chosen a negative that is correctly exposed, is in focus, and needs no cropping (cutting off an area of the print by masking it off the easel). The first step, then, is to place the negative in the negative carrier of the enlarger, which holds the negative flat in the enlarger. The emulsion side (dull side) of the negative should be face down, toward the lens. If the negative is not face down, then the print will be backwards ("flopped"). Since some enlargers can handle different sizes of negatives, they will have different sizes of negative carriers. Be sure to use the right negative carrier for the size of film you are working with.

Some carriers sandwich the negative between two pieces of glass. If you are using this type, be sure not to handle the glass surfaces, as fingerprints will cause uneven lighting and a loss of sharpness in your print.

Once the negative is in the carrier, it must be cleaned carefully. Even a negative carefully filed in an envelope will inevitably gather some dust. Unless this dust or lint is removed, it will cause little white spots in the print. To remove dust, use either a soft camel's hair brush or a can of compressed air. If you use a brush, be sure to brush both sides of the negative. If your negative carrier has glass in the openings, clean all sides of the glass prior to inserting the negative. This is to remove all dust on the glass itself. When using air, point the nozzle with the snorkel tip at the negative and press the spray button.

After all dust is removed, place the negative in the enlarger immediately, so that no new dust will settle on it. In order to insert the negative carrier on some enlargers, you must raise the lamp housing of the enlarger. Usually the carrier will lock into a tight position, indicating that it is in place. The lamp housing can now be brought back down on the carrier. Always do this with the enlarger off, so that the enlarger light will not spill out into the darkroom and ruin someone else's paper. To provide a better viewing surface and compensate for the thickness of the photographic paper, place a sheet of white paper in the enlarging easel during focusing. When the carrier is in place and the blank paper on the easel, the enlarger can be turned on to focus the image and set the size of the print. First, open the iris on the enlarging lens as wide as possible for easier viewing. Next, raise and lower the enlarger body on the vertical column until the image is the desired size. Focus the negative by turning the knob on the enlarger until the image on the easel looks sharp. If the size changes, you may have to readjust both the height of the enlarger and the focus. Then you are ready to make the exposure.

Print Exposure

The exposure time in enlarging varies with the density of the negative, the size of the enlargement, the paper being used, the lens opening on the enlarger, and the enlarger itself. Because there are so many different variables, it is best always to work with the same enlarger and to keep the lens set at a certain f-stop. Since a flat negative is being enlarged on another flat surface, depth of field is generally not a problem in enlarging. Generally, there is no need to close the iris on the lens all the way down, since this only decreases the amount of light projected. A lens should be closed all the way only when a very light (thin) negative is being enlarged. Otherwise, keep the lens opening constant at about f/8 or f/11.

Making a Test Print

A major consideration in printing a negative is how dark the print should be. This is a visual judgment. Making a test print will help you determine which exposure time will work best for a particular negative. First put the negative in the carrier and adjust the enlarger for size and focus. Then insert a sheet of paper in the easel. If a timer is being used, set it for 25 seconds.

In this test, a number of exposures are made on a single sheet of paper. To make the test strips, cover all of your enlarging paper

1 enlarger
2 timer
3 focusing knob
4 enlarging knob
5 negative carrier
6 enlarger base
7 lens

optional equipment
8 micro focus finder
9 enlarging easel

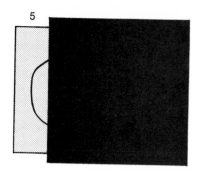

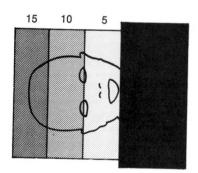

with an opaque sheet of cardboard except for a strip a little over an inch wide. Expose the paper for five seconds. Now move the cardboard down another inch and expose the paper for another five seconds. Repeat this procedure until you have gone through five successive exposures of five seconds each (with your enlarging lens set at f/8 or f/11). The result should be a full piece of enlarging paper with a series of strips exposed for multiples of five seconds. The first strip exposed (the top one) will have had a cumulative exposure of 25 seconds, the next 20 seconds, the third 15 seconds, and so on down the paper.

In the first photo, which shows the first exposure, notice that four-fifths of the paper is covered by the cardboard. The second photograph is the third exposure. Here, notice that the cardboard has been moved three-fifths of the way down. After the last exposure is completed, develop and examine the print.

After examining the five exposures, you will probably find that the last two exposures (at 10 and 5 seconds) are too light; the first exposure (at 25 seconds) will probably be too dark. The correct exposure for this negative appears to be between 15 and 20 seconds. However, this is a matter of taste.

If this set of exposures is not suitable, then increase or decrease the exposure time for each strip. If all the strips were too dark, then shorten the intervals to two seconds each. If all the strips were too light, increase the amount of time. Lighter negatives need less exposure time because light passes through them more quickly. A darker (denser) negative needs more time, as light takes longer to penetrate. An exposure of more than 40 seconds indicates that your negative is overexposed. In this case, you may have to set the lens on the enlarger at its maximum opening.

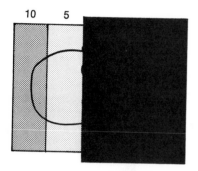

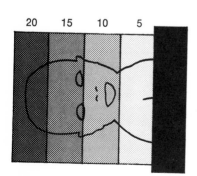

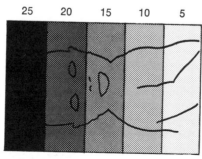

Space out exposures uniformly in order to facilitate selection of proper exposure.

Full Print Exposure

Once you have established exposure time by making the test print, you can print the entire negative. Follow the same procedures as before—be sure that the negative is clean and the chemicals are fresh. Do not move the easel holding the paper during the exposure, as this may blur the image. Also be careful not to hit the enlarger, as it will vibrate and cause a blurred image. Make sure that your hands are clean and dry. Any chemicals on them will stain the paper.

Entire image was exposed at 20 seconds.

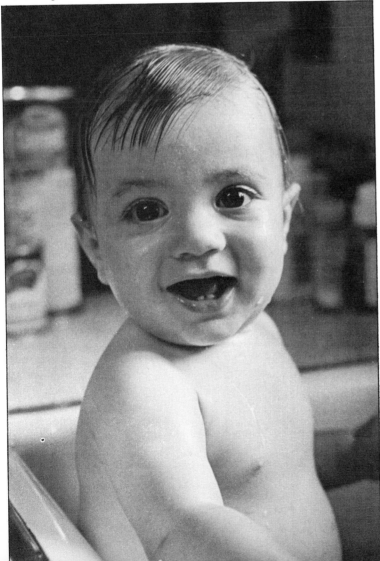

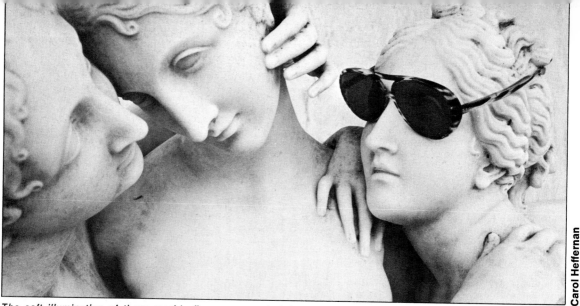

The soft illumination of these marble figures suggested the use of a low contrast paper to maintain the subtlety of the subject.

Photographic Papers

As stated earlier, photographic paper is classified according to five different qualities: (1) tone, (2) surface, (3) speed, (4) contrast, and (5) thickness. Of these, the most important is contrast.

Contrast is the comparison of values (light and dark) in a negative or print. Contrast in a negative is determined by exposure and development. An overexposed or overdeveloped negative is too dense—it has too much contrast. An underexposed or underdeveloped negative is too light—it looks "flat." In other words, there is not enough contrast between the lights and the darks.

Photographic paper is made in six contrast levels (grades), to allow for the many variations in negatives. For example, a negative that is contrasty to start with is printed on a paper that will decrease the differences in tone, making it look normal. On the other hand, a negative that looks flat would be printed on a contrasty paper. Papers are numbered from 1 to 6, indicating the level of contrast. Number 1 paper is the least contrasty; number 2 is for well-exposed negatives (normal); number 3 paper is used for slightly flat negatives; number 4 for flat negatives; number 5 paper for very thin negatives; and finally, number 6 is for those negatives that are extremely underexposed and lack any detail.

A number of paper manufacturers, including Eastman Kodak, are introducing a new system to indicate the various contrast levels by description, not number. Although this system is used primarily for RC (resin-coated) paper, it may eventually replace the present system of numbers. The conversion table is: soft (#1 paper), medium (#2), hard (#3), extra hard (#4), and ultra hard (#5).

Low contrast would not have been appropriate for this photo of a dramatic event.

Another type of paper available allows for seven different contrast ranges with the use of filters. It is "variable contrast paper," the most popular brand being Kodak's Polycontrast.® A variable contrast paper eliminates the need to buy several grades of paper. Instead, the contrast is changed by inserting a filter in the enlarger, usually under the lens. These filters are numbered 1, 1½, 2, 2½, 3, 3½, 4, corresponding to the levels of contrast. Variable contrast paper also allows intermediate contrast levels (like 1½), which cannot be achieved with regular stock paper. When variable contrast paper is used, the exposure time must be readjusted for the different filters, for each increase in contrast also increases the density of the filter. Since the light passing through the negative must also pass through the filter, exposure time must be increased with the darker filters.

Photographers sometimes confuse exposure with contrast. For instance, after making a test print in which all of the strips are too light, a beginning photographer may change to a lower contrast paper. This is the wrong thing to do. If a test strip is too light, then the exposure time should be increased. Then, after a new test, decide whether the print has too much or too little contrast. There is no rule of thumb governing contrast selection. However, if after a test print has been made with a correct exposure strip and developed for the proper length of time, the image is still stark white and black, then the contrast grade is too high. If the strip has an overall gray ("muddy") look to it, then the contrast grade was too low. The eye is the best judge of proper contrast.

One of the unique qualities of photography is its ability to capture a scene in its complete tonal range. In photography, tonal range is the scale of values ranging from white through a wide range of grays to black. Tonal range is best if the negative is properly exposed and then printed on a number 1 or 2 paper. The use of a higher contrast paper will result in a loss of tonal range. This effect may be desirable if the negative has too much of an overall grey look, that is, if it lacks contrast to begin with. In other words, the lower the contrast of the paper, the greater the tonal range—the greater the number of gray tones it can reproduce. The higher the contrast of the paper, the shorter the tonal range—the fewer the number of gray tones it is capable of reproducing.

Sometimes a photograph can be printed successfully on different contrast grades of paper. As the photographs show, each print communicates a slightly different conception of the same negative. (See photos on facing page.) In the first print, the image is "realistically" portrayed with a long gradation of tone. This print, if not seen with the others, would be considered technically good. In the second print, the contrast was increased a grade. Notice that a few of the grays have disappeared from the subject. But notice, too, that the image is visually more exciting than the first. Is the photographer communicating more with this print? The third photograph was printed on a number 6 paper. Almost all the gray scale is gone. It has become a "graphic" interpretation—a much colder, harsher rendering of the same scene. The contrast in each of the prints influences the way we respond to them. No single print is "better" than the others. Some people may like the first print best while others may prefer the renderings with more dramatic contrasts. From a technical standpoint, the first print would be considered the best. However, printing is not only a matter of technical considerations. The photographer must also consider what he or she wants to communicate. In the end, it is the photographer's point of view we see when we look at a photograph.

The tone of a photographic paper is described in terms of being "warm" or "cold." A warm-tone paper is one in which the blacks are brownish. A cold-tone paper is one in which the blacks are blue. Corresponding warm-tone and cold-tone developers are made for use with these different papers. Cold-tone papers are used for the most types of photography. Popular brands include Kodak's Polycontrast® and Kodabromide,® Afga's Brovira,® and Ilford's Ilfobrom.® Warm-tone papers have traditionally been used for portrait work. Such papers include Kodak's Medalist,® Portralure,® and Ektalure.® The tone of a paper can also be changed by the use of a paper toner such as sepia (warm brown), selenium (red-brown), blue, and red. When using a toner, it is best to start with a warm-tone paper.

The surfaces of photographic papers also vary. Because photographers have different tastes and produce photographs for many different purposes, Kodak alone offers 11 different paper surfaces. Generally, it is best to use either an F (glossy), J (high

realistic rendition of gray tones

contrast is increased

very high contrast

lustre), or N (smooth) surface. These papers will not texture the photographic image. The F-surface paper is most generally used. This paper can be dried face up in the dryer or, to produce a high gloss, can be dried with the surface facing the drum. The latter process is called ferrotyping. For ferrotyping, the drum or surface of the dryer must be extremely clean. The print is placed face down on the drum, with the excess water removed and rolled down with a print roller. If there is air between the surface of the drum and the print, the print will dry unevenly and look spotty.

One paper that has a high gloss without ferrotyping is RC (resin-coated) F-surface. RC paper dries quickly and should not be put in an electric dryer. Simply squeeze down the print and then either place it in a blotter roll, where it will dry in ten minutes, or lay it on a clean surface in open air. An RC print will not curl as other photographic paper does. Variable contrast (Polycontrast®) RC paper in both F and N surfaces is also available.

Speeds of photo paper also vary. Contact paper is generally less sensitive to light than enlarging paper. However, enlarging papers vary in speed from brand to brand. Polycontrast,® for example, is made in either a "rapid" or a "normal" speed. The cold-tone papers usually are faster than their warm-tone counterparts. Whenever the type of paper is changed (such as going from Kodabromide® to Medalist),® the exposure time must also be readjusted.

Finally, as mentioned earlier, there are three different paper weights or thicknesses—single weight, medium weight, and double weight. Double weight paper is about twice as thick as single weight and also about a third as expensive. However, double weight papers work best for very large prints (11" x 14", 16" x 20") because these prints have a tendency to curl. When beginning photography, it is best to use single weight paper to keep costs down. RC papers are available only in medium weight.

unmanipulated print

Corrective Manipulations

In theory, a well-exposed negative should produce a print with a long tonal range. However, this is not always the case. Film is capable of recording more subtleties in tone than can be printed. For instance, a light area in your negative may contain some detail, but if the exposure is based on the rest of the negative, that area will turn completely black in the print. If the exposure is timed to hold the detail in that light area, then the print will be too light.

In another negative, just the opposite may be true. A dense area of the negative contains detail visible to your eye, but a print based on the overall exposure makes that area completely white in the print. If the exposure is changed to gain back the detail in the dark area of the negative, the rest of the print will be too dark. There are two techniques you can use to change such areas in a print—"burning in" and "dodging." "Burning in" will darken an area, while "dodging" will lighten it.

To burn in an area, you must block out the rest of the picture while allowing more light to fall on the area you want to make darker. To do this, first determine the correct exposure based on the entire picture area. Then take a sheet of opaque cardboard and make a hole in the middle of it. Place this cardboard between the lens of the enlarger and the paper. With the hole over the area to be darkened, turn the enlarger light on and re-expose the part of the print that needs to be made darker. Move the cardboard about constantly, in a random way, or final print may show the burned-in area as a dark round circle. Move the cardboard closer to the lens to increase the size of the area covered or closer to the paper for a smaller area.

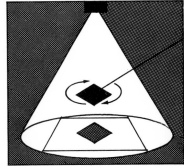

dodge an area to lighten

Dodging an area will lighten it. In other words, keeping light from the area will cause it to print lighter than it normally would. You can make a tool for dodging by cutting various shapes out of cardboard and fastening them to wires. The wire handles make it possible to dodge out areas near the center of the photograph without blocking out light near the edges. When dodging an area, it is important to keep the tool in constant motion so that the area blends in with the rest of the print. If a large area is to be dodged, your hand can be used to block off a portion of the light.

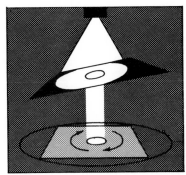

burn in an area to darken

Timing either of these techniques is a matter of trial and error. As your experience increases, you will be able to determine more quickly the correct times for dodging or burning in.

Cropping an image will not be necessary if you have composed the image carefully in the viewfinder of the camera. However, sometimes it is desirable. One way to crop the image is to use larger paper than you want for your final print. Once the image is printed, the unwanted area is cut off. Another method is to blow up the image in the enlarger so that the unwanted portion of the negative is outside the area of the enlarging paper. You may also move the arms of the paper easel (if you are using the adjustable type) so that the unwanted area is masked out. Cropping should be a last resort. The larger an image, the less sharpness it has. Your cropped image will not be as sharp as a full negative print. You should learn to compose with the camera: if you take the picture five different ways or from five different viewpoints, cropping should not be necessary.

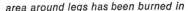

area around legs has been burned in

Vignetting is a combination of the above manipulations. You normally use it when you want to single out one area of the negative. Use the same cut-out cardboard tool that you made for "burning in." In this case, though, make only one exposure, with the hole over the area you want pictured. Keep the cardboard in constant motion during the exposure. When the print is developed, the subject will appear with everything around it fading off to pure white. Vignetting can be used when you have a portrait photograph with an unattractive or cluttered background.

A less common problem is that of distortion. For instance, if you photograph a tall building, the lines of the building tend to

lean toward the center of your picture. This is a perspective problem, and usually you can do nothing to correct for it when taking the picture unless you use a view camera. However, in enlarging, "distortion correction" can save most of these pictures. To do this, raise one end of the enlarging easel about one or two inches. Then, after focusing on the halfway point of the image, close down the lens of the enlarger all the way, so that you achieve the greatest depth of field. This is one of the few times that closing a lens down all the way has any real function in enlarging.

Other manipulative processes also can be done in the darkroom. For instance, you can intentionally add texture to a photograph by the use of texture screens. You can make a sharp image look diffused or soft, and you can print more than one negative at a time. These last techniques generally do not enhance a good photograph, but only cheapen it. Gimmicks are no substitute for a creative statement. There is really only one way to make a good photograph, and that is by taking a good photograph. You can make a good photograph look better by burning in or dodging, but you can't make a bad photograph look good.

Problems in Printing

The photographs on these two pages illustrate problems that may occur in printing. The following are suggested ways to avoid them.

White cracks are caused by mishandling a wet print. Only touch the white border area of the print. Handle it carefully.

Out-of-focus prints have several causes. The paper may not have been in perfect contact with the negative in contact printing. Or, in enlarging, the negative may not have been focused properly, or the enlarger may have vibrated during the exposure. Make sure that the negative is in fine focus, and never touch the enlarger during exposure.

careless handling

out of focus

overexposed

underexposed

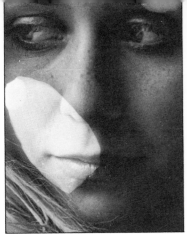
contaminated hands

too flat

uneven development

muddy print

If a print becomes too dark in the developer, reduce the amount of exposure. If it turns completely black within a few seconds after it is immersed in the developer, cut the exposure time in half.

If the print is too light, increase the amount of exposure. If it is completely white after two minutes in the developer, double the amount of exposure.

If a white fingerprint shows up on a print, it may be caused either by a fingerprint on the negative or by handling the paper with hypo on your hands. A dark fingerprint usually means the paper was handled with developer on the hands before exposure. Always keep your hands clean and dry.

A flat print has no pure whites or deep blacks. It results from using the wrong contrast paper. The contrast should be increased by at least one grade.

A muddy print has a very poor tonal range. Again, there are no strong whites or blacks, just an overall gray. Muddiness is usually caused by overexposure and by pulling the print out of the developer too soon. Readjust the exposure so that the print remains in the developer for at least 1½ minutes.

Black marks on a print are usually caused by deep scratches or pinholes in the negative. Always handle your negatives with care.

White spots are usually caused by dirt or lint on the negative. Always clean your negative before making a print.

Uneven development indicates that the entire print was not immersed in the developer at the same time. Be careful to immerse the print all at once and to agitate it right away.

Presenting Your Photographs

By viewing other people's work, we judge how they see. We judge how they see a scene through their composition. We judge their

dirty negative

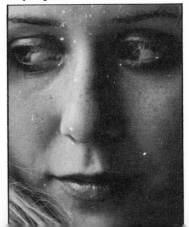

borderless print

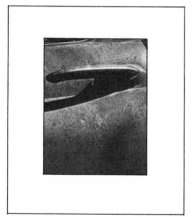

matted print with borders

craftsmanship by the way the photograph is printed. And we also judge the effort made to display their photograph. If the photograph is loose and unmounted, we have a good idea that the photographer didn't care about other people seeing his or her work or was just too lazy to do anything about it. If, on the other hand, the print is clean and well mounted, we judge the photographer with more respect. If you, the photographer, want other people to respect your work, you must respect it yourself. This section, therefore, will deal with the presentation of a photograph—the final touches.

After the print is in the wash water, check it to make sure that there are no white or dark spots on it. If the print is covered with lint, then go no further. It's time to remake the print. However, almost any print will have a few little white or dark spots on it. These spots can usually be taken care of by a technique known as "spotting." White spots on prints are usually the result of dust or fingerprints on the negative. Small white streaks on the print are usually due to light scratches on the shiny side of the film. Because dust, lint, fingerprints, and surface scratches on the negative prevent light from passing through, they appear white in the print.

In spotting a print, you add a mixture of black dye and water to the white area to make it blend in with the rest of the photograph. This dye is a commercial product known as SpoTone,® which is available in three different colors of black, numbers 1, 2, and 3. Numbers 1 and 2 are used for warm-tone paper; number 3 is for cold-tone spotting. Besides the SpoTone, you need a fine camel's hair brush (grade 0 or 00), a palette for mixing, and a container of water.

The dry print is placed on a clean surface to avoid getting dirt on it. The water and dye are mixed on the palette with the brush. To make sure that the tone of black is about the same as the area surrounding the white, brush a small amount of it on a piece of blank white paper. Compare the color with the print. If it is too dark, then add more water to the mixture. If it is too light, then add more SpoTone. Once the proper tone has been reached, apply it to the white area. Application of the SpoTone to the print is not like painting a water color. It is not brushed on, but placed dot by dot over the white area. Care is important, because if the SpoTone spills over the confines of the spot, it looks worse. One other thing to avoid when spotting is getting too much moisture on the tip of the brush. In this case, the drop of SpoTone will again spill over the white area. Remember, SpoTone is permanent, so use only a little at a time. It cannot be removed if you add too much.

Black spots on negatives occur because of scratches on the emulsion of the negative or air bubbles during film development. Black spots are usually more difficult to remove than white spots. To begin with, the black spot has to be bleached white. To do this, use a toothpick with cotton wrapped around it and dip it into ordinary laundry-bleach or farmers reducer. Apply the solution to the dark spot until it turns white. This will usually take a few applications. Once the spot is white, use the dye as descibed above to tone it back down to normal.

Mounting a Photograph

After the print has been spotted, it is ready for the final stage of presentation—fastening it to the mount board. The first reason for mounting a print is that a photograph is otherwise difficult to keep flat. A print that has curled is hard to look at, and trying to flatten it may crack the emulsion. Second, a photograph looks better if it is mounted on a stiff board.

The Dry Mount Press. Dry mount tissue is usually a shellac-impregnated sheet that is placed between the photograph and the board. When pressed with even heat in the dry mount press, the shellac melts and forms a permanent bond between the photo and the board. Dry mounting must be done quickly and carefully. If normal photographic paper (not RC paper) is to be mounted, the temperature of the press should be set at 275°F. For RC paper, the temperature of the press should not be over 150°F. RC paper also requires the use of a special type of mounting tissue, such as

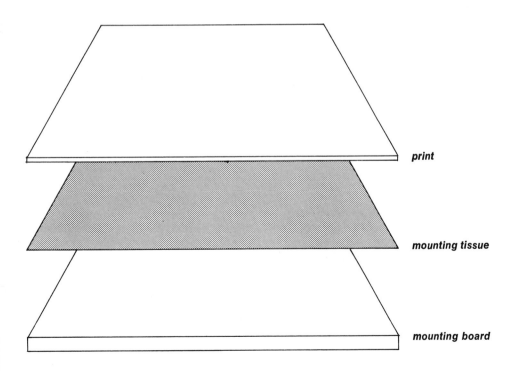

print

mounting tissue

mounting board

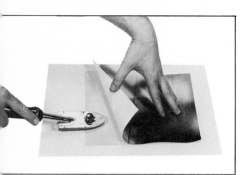

When borders are desired, position mounting tissue before tacking tissue down.

Kodak Type II® tissue or Seal Colormount® tissue. Normal papers can use Seal MT-5® tissue or Admeco® tissue. Do not use mounting tissue meant for normal paper when attempting RC mounting, or RC tissue for mounting normal paper. They will not work and may ruin your photographs.

After the temperature of the press has been set for the type of paper being mounted, attach the tissue to the back of the print, using a tacking iron. To begin, you place the print face down on a clean surface; lay a sheet of tissue on it, aligning at least two edges; and stick the tissue down with the tacking iron by making a short stroke in the center of the back. Then you trim off the white borders of the prints. It is important that none of the tissue extends beyond the photograph after it is trimmed. If it does, the photograph will stick in the dry mount press. Trim the photograph with a paper cutter or use a metal ruler and cut along its edge with a razor blade.

There are several ways to mount a photograph on a board. In the first method, the print is mounted on a white board so that white borders show (other colors can be used, although they generally distract from the photograph). First, place the trimmed print face up on the board. Space the print on the board so that the borders are about the same width on at least two sides. The print may have more space on the bottom than on the top. For a 5" x 7" print, for example, a good border would be about 3 inches on the top and sides and about 3½ inches on the bottom. After spacing, a corner of the photograph is lifted slightly and the tissue is stuck to the board with the tacking iron. Be sure that the iron never touches the surface of the print. If it does, the heat and the shellac left on the iron will ruin the photo.

The photograph is now ready to be inserted into the press. Place the board, print side up, on the pad of the press and cover the face of the print with a large, clean sheet of paper. It is important to cover the entire surface of the photograph with paper, since the print must never touch the heated metal of the press. The time that the press remains closed on the print will depend on the weight of the board, the press being used, the thickness of the cover sheet, and the type of tissue. Check the instructions on the tissue package or experiment a little. Generally, though, it is between 15 and 30 seconds.

Another popular method of mounting is called "bleed mounting." In this method, the white borders of the board are trimmed so that the edges of the board and the print are flush. After the print is mounted in the usual way, the borders of the board are cut off using a metal straight-edge (ruler) and a mat knife. Be sure you have a sharp blade, or your cut will be ragged. Do not attempt to cut through both the print and board in one stroke. Rather, use a series of light strokes until the excess border is separated. Don't try to pull apart a partially cut board as it will leave an unsightly rough edge.

Practice mounting unwanted prints.

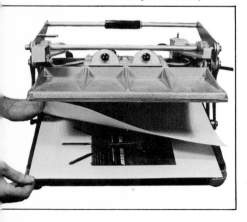

Problems in Mounting

The problems that occur frequently in mounting are dirt particles under the mounted print, air bubbles, and the print not sticking to the board.

Dirt is the easiest problem to take care of. *Always* keep the print covered and carefully stored until you're ready to mount it. Don't let it sit on a dirty counter. If specks of dirt get trapped under the print after it's been mounted, they appear as little lumps in the surface. At that point, you can do little except try to press them down with the flat side of a fingernail. If you press too hard, you'll make a "pimple" on your print.

Air bubbles appear as blisters on the print. They are usually caused by moisture in the board. If the problem occurs often, place the bare board in the press for a few seconds before tacking the photograph down on it. As a remedy for those prints that do have air bubbles, you may try puncturing the bubble with a pin, through the back of the board, and reheating it.

Finally, if the print comes loose from the tissue, but the tissue is stuck to the board, it indicates that too much heat was used or the print was in the press too long. Usually the only solution is to remount the print on a fresh board.

Assignment: Basic Enlarging

1. When you are "burning in" an area in a print, are you giving that area more or less time than the rest of the print? If an area needs burning in, is that area in the negative too light or too dark? Explain. How would you answer these questions if you were "dodging" rather than burning in? Explain.

2. Suppose you are making an enlargement and the correct exposure is 10 seconds at $f/8$. How will the exposure time be affected if the lens opening is changed to $f/5.6$? —to $f/11$? Explain.

3. If a negative is not sharp (out of focus), can you improve the focus by stopping down the enlarging lens to the smallest f-stop to get maximum depth of field? Explain. If the negative is warped, will it improve the sharpness of the print to stop the lens down? Explain.

4. What are all of the factors that affect the exposure time of an enlargement?

5. Should a high contrast negative be printed on a high contrast paper and a low contrast negative on a low contrast paper? Explain.

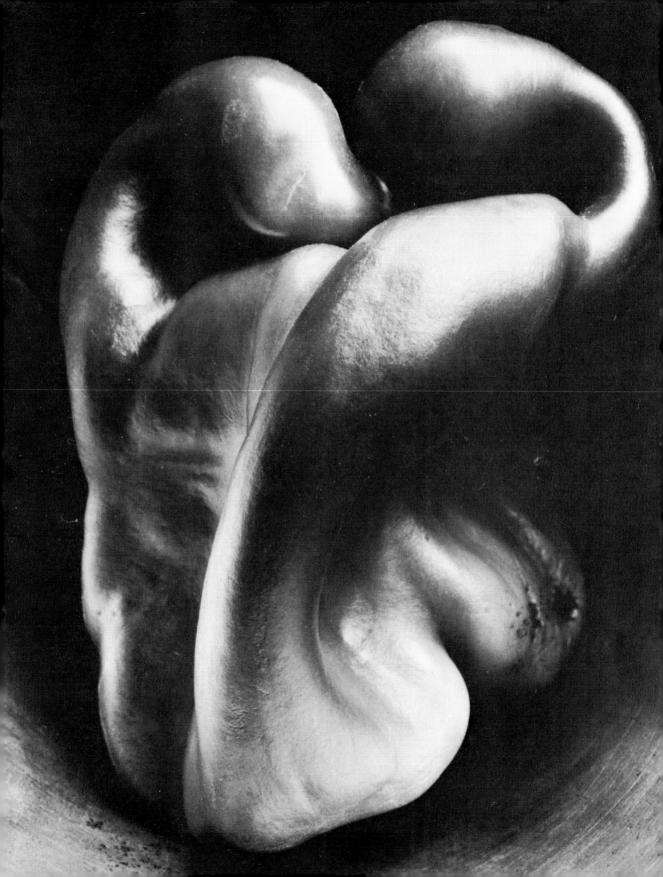

Visual Aspects of Photography

7

The goal of all photographers is to make a good photograph. But what is a good photograph? No two photographers will agree on all the elements that make a photograph good. For this reason it is hard to judge a photograph, since there is no complete agreement on the criteria for judging it. As in most arts, the critic's viewpoint and personality usually determine what is "good" and what is not.

It is easy to say "I like this photograph; it is good." It is just as easy to say "I don't like this photograph; it is bad." In both cases the viewer has made a judgment about the photograph. But this judgment is useful only if the viewer says "I don't like the photograph *because* . . ." or "I like the photograph *because* . . ."

Before we look at that key word "because," we have to understand the nature and purpose of photography. Like drawing or painting, it is a visual medium. Like other artists, photographers usually want their pictures to be seen by other people; so photography is also a form of communication. However, unless the photographer has something worthwhile to communicate, his or her effort is wasted.

Those who are successful in using photography to communicate do not simply look at the world—they *see* it. And they see it within the limitations of the camera's viewfinder.

Communication is a two-way proposition. The photographer has seen something he or she wants to share with someone else, and the viewer is presumed to be willing to view it and thereby share it. The viewer must be open to the stimulus of the photograph, while the photographer must supply a strong, satisfying statement.

If we, as photographers, can define the purpose of our photographs, the better chance there is for the viewer to respond to them. If we, as viewers, understand more about photography, our judgments will have more validity.

Although there is no complete set of values for determining what makes a good photograph, a good photograph will probably have certain qualities that may be either technical or esthetic. The *technical* aspect refers to how the photograph was taken and printed. The *esthetic* aspect is the visual impact or appeal of the photograph. These qualities may, and do, overlap.

Edward Weston (*Mark Jacobs Collection*)   81

Since a photograph is also a form of communication, it must have something to say. And the more clearly the message is stated, the more likely the viewer is to understand it. Very often this clarity of statement depends on technique, which begins with the camera and ends in the darkroom.

The photographer must always be in full control of the camera. He or she must know the exact exposure, in terms of *f* stop and shutter speed, that will achieve the desired effect. Depth of field, for example, can be used to create either an indefinite plane of sharpness or one that gradually falls off into a blur. However, unless the photographer knows how to control depth of field, taking a photograph will be a haphazard venture. A good photographer is able to *repeat* a photograph.

In the darkroom, the photographer must know how to print, what grade of paper to use, and what exposure to give the paper. Technique in itself will not make a good photograph. However, poor technique will diminish an otherwise excellent photograph.

Eugene Smith

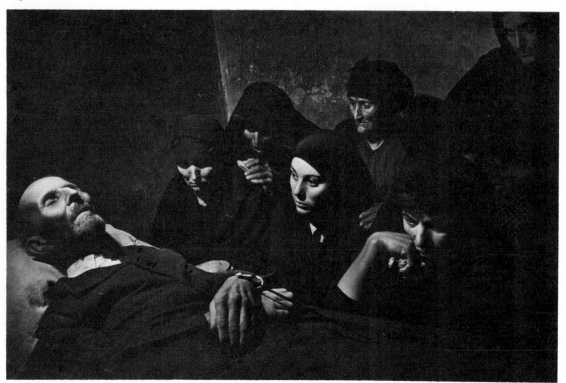

Edward Steichen *(Art Institute of Chicago, Alfred Stieglitz Collection)*

Jerry Uelsman

The ability to see is the photographer's most important qualification. Would you have seen the tree in this photograph, or would you have walked by the tree without seeing the possibility for a good picture? Seeing means perceiving the visual elements and shape relationships around you. After seeing a subject suitable for a photograph, the photographer will start to visualize that subject as it could be presented in a print.

How we see and what we see constitute the photographer's vision, the photographer's eye. We look at many things in our lives. A building, for instance, is a structure that takes up a certain amount of space and we look at it in relation to the other buildings around it, to the sidewalk and street, the traffic, etc. However, do we see the texture of the sides of the building? Do we see the shadow it casts? Do we see the reflections in its windows? Because there is often much more to a familiar object that we realize, the photographer must be able to see everyday objects in a personal, visual context, rather than just as objects.

People are popular subjects for photographs. Yet how many of us really look closely at them? Very few of us take a picture of a person who is working; we usually wait until people are home, sitting in a comfortable chair, waiting to have their picture taken. Also, people have hands, feet, legs, a back, and ears. Why take pictures only of their face? Moreover, most of us avoid people we don't like to look at. We don't take a picture of someone who doesn't appeal to our personal sense of beauty—despite whatever merits such a picture might have.

Unfortunately, most pictures of people are snapshots, taken by the millions by people with all types of cameras and all degrees of skill. Snapshots are essentially souvenirs for the photographer—records of places, things, or people. Seldom do they communicate to a wide audience. The difference between the snapshot and the photograph can be stated in terms of purpose. Also, a snapshot is taken in haste; a photograph requires time. The time that is needed to get a good photograph is due, in part, to the time required for visualizing the subject.

The main point of most snapshots is to record something the photographer wants to remember. But subject matter is not the most important aspect of a good photograph. A good photograph expresses a viewpoint. A photograph of a wall is not necessarily less important than a photograph of a person.

Most novice photographers think they must go out and take pictures of people or landmarks or other familiar things. Such pictures usually turn out to be nothing more than sophisticated snapshots. For instance, a picture of the Empire State Building probably will not be important, but simply a sophisticated snapshot. You must control the subject, rather than let it control you.

Many novice photographers, again, are preoccupied with the content of their photographs: the "who" or "where" or "what"

Arthur Rothstein *(FSA photograph, Mark Jacobs Collection)*

they are picturing. While these may be important in some types of photographs, especially in photojournalism, they are not important for the learning or beginning photographer.

"Then what shall I photograph?" Anything you want to. There are no rules about subject matter. Photograph anything that in-

Patrice Grimbert

terests you, whether it be a pencil, a burnt cigarette, a wall, a window, a face, or a piece of wood.

Just about everything has been photographed; so don't be compelled to "discover" a new subject. Rather, try to find something you are interested in, not something you think you *should* be in-

terested in. Also try to find a new way of seeing a subject. For instance, if you usually see a subject from a certain angle, try moving to a different position and seeing it from a different angle. Try photographing the subject from a lower vantage point—perhaps your knees. Or look down on the subject by standing on a ladder. Find the way that appeals to you visually—which may take a long time. Whatever way you choose, don't be afraid to try it.

As an experiment, you might take an unloaded camera (so you won't worry about wasting film) and simply walk around the city or park "seeing" subjects. Walk up to strange people, or plants, or animals and "take" a photograph. Discover for yourself that the world is full of subjects.

Now you may be thinking "Okay, I can shoot anything I want to. But how should I photograph it?" Again, this depends entirely upon you, and upon your knowledge of your camera. For instance, you can portray motion in at least two ways. You can (1) freeze the subject with a fast shutter speed or you can (2) blur the subject by using a slow shutter speed. Neither way is more "correct" than the other. However, each will create a different impression of the subject.

Sharpness is another factor you can control. (There is no rule that a picture *has* to be sharp.) Focus sharply on a subject and take a photo. Then turn the lens so that the image is slightly out of focus and take another shot. Try again, with the image completely out of focus. You may like one of your out-of-focus shots better than the one that is sharp. If your picture is visually exciting, you've achieved part of the goal.

As we said earlier, good technique alone does not make a good photograph, but a good photograph cannot be made without it. Technical skill is a necessary starting point for taking good photographs. Poor technique will interfere with the statement you want to make. A photograph's visual impact is created by its esthetic composition, but it is technique that conveys the message.

After choosing your subject and deciding the technical details, you must come to grips with the visual impact the photograph will produce. Determine how the subject matter looks to you and how you will interpret it. Consider its obvious visual attributes, such as shape and texture. (Carefully examine the photograph on the left. By this time, you know that photo paper is basically smooth, yet this picture is inviting to the touch. It also appeals to a sense *other* than sight.) Shape and texture, by themselves, may not create an interesting photograph. They can, however, create a pattern. Thus shape and texture must be organized into a *composition* that will determine the photograph's visual impact.

Composition in a photograph is the esthetic arrangement of shapes and space. Again, there are no rules that determine a good composition. Every photograph is made for a different purpose and by a different technique. According to photographer Edward Weston:

Now to consult rules of composition before making a picture is a little like consulting the law of gravitation before going out for a walk. . . . When subject matter is forced to fit a preconceived pattern, there can be no freshness of vision. Following rules of composition can only lead to a tedious repetition of pictorial clichés.

For the moment, let us assume that every photograph that communicates an idea or thought has some structure or composition. How does the photographer achieve it? One photographer, Henri Cartier-Bresson, thinks in terms of repeating geometric shapes—rhythm:

Author

> If a photograph is to communicate its subject in all its intensity, the relationships of form must be rigorously established. Photography implies the recognition of a rhythm in the world of real things. . . . In a photograph, composition is the result of a simultaneous coalition, the organic coordination of elements seen by the eye.

The viewer's eye is lured into the photograph by the repeated shapes. This kind of rhythm can create a sense of order and unity in a photograph even if the forms are different. In this photograph of a street, rhythm is created by the repeated white lines.

Balance—the relationship between objects in a photograph—is another element of composition. Balance can be achieved very obviously, as by having two identical shapes in a photograph. However, balance does not necessarily depend on exactly matching sizes and shapes. It may be helpful to think of a fulcrum that balances different-size objects within a composition: two objects of different size will balance if the smaller one is farther from the fulcrum. For extremely subtle balance, study the arrangement of objects in a mobile.

Lights and darks (tonal values) also are important factors in composing a picture. Highlights (whites) are an effective device for drawing the viewer's eye into the photograph. However, highlights can also be ineffective: light areas at the edge of a photo will draw the eye out of the picture. This is because light areas tend to project a photograph, whereas dark areas recede. Dark areas can also isolate a subject.

When dealing with any camera image, it is important to remember that you are "translating" a three-dimensional subject into a two-dimensional representation. Also, you must become aware of the relationship between negative and positive space. No part of a photograph can be wasted. A "weak" area, occupying a certain amount of space in a photograph, will destroy the harmony of the composition. All areas of a photo, dark or light, geometric or free flowing, must work together to create a feeling of design. There is no formula in composition. Again, Edward Weston put it quite eloquently:

Stieglitz *(Art Institute of Chicago, Alfred Stieglitz Collection)*

Karsh, Ottawa

91

Good composition is only the strongest way of seeing a subject. It cannot be taught because, like all creative effort, it is a matter of personal growth.

Every composition is a response to the subject. A good photographer will respond to the subject emotionally and intellectually. And a good photograph will clearly elicit that response. Ansel Adams states it this way:

A great photograph is a full expression of what one feels about what is being photographed in the deepest sense, and is, thereby, a true expression of what one feels about life in its entirety.

Photographer Paul Strand sums it up very nicely:

In closing, I will say this to you as students of photography. Don't think when I say "students" that I am trying to talk down.

Walker Evans *(FSA photograph, Mark Jacobs Collection)*

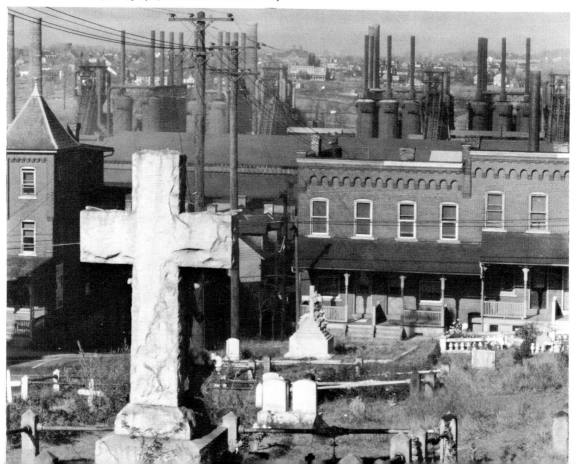

We are all students, including Stieglitz. Some a little longer at it than others, a little more experienced. When you cease to be a student you might as well be dead as far as the significance of your work is concerned. So I am simply talking to you as one student to others, out of my own experience. And I say to you, before you give your time, and you will have to give much, to photography, find out in yourselves how much it means to you. If you really want to paint, then do not photograph except as you may want to amuse yourselves along with the rest of Mr. Eastman's customers. Photography is not a shortcut to painting, being an artist, or anything else. On the other hand, if this camera machine with its materials fascinates you, compels your energy and respect, learn to photograph. Find out just what this machine and these materials can do without any interference except your own vision. Photograph a tree, a machine, a table, any old thing; do it over and over again under different conditions of light. See what your negative will record.

Assignment: Visual Aspects of Photography

1. What is the difference between a photograph and a snapshot? Give examples of situations that are more likely to produce either "snapshots" or photographs. What is the difference in the attitude or intention of the person using the camera to take a "snapshot"? —a "photograph"?
2. What is the difference between "technique" and "esthetics" as they apply to visual communication in photography? Can you explain how these two overlap and work in combination to produce a good photograph? Try to find an example of a photograph which is technically excellent but lacking in esthetic interest. Find a photograph that has esthetic potential, but whose excellence is harmed by poor technique. Refer to specific points about these two photographs as you explain the relationship between technique and esthetics.
3. Find an example of a photograph in which a common, even overdone, subject has been shown in a new and interesting way through the unique viewpoint of the photographer.
4. Edward Weston states that "following rules of composition can only lead to a tedious repetition of pictorial clichés." What is a pictorial cliché? Can you think of any pictorial clichés? Go through sources of photographs, such as magazines, newspapers, and advertising and try to find examples of what you would consider pictorial clichés.

*Quotes from "Photographers on Photography." Edited by Nathan Lyons, Prentice-Hall, Inc., 1966, Englewood Cliffs, New Jersey.

Film and Filters

8

Photographic film is a relatively recent invention in the history of photography. For many years prior to the introduction of film in 1887, glass plates were used instead. In fact, many scientists and technicians today still use photographic glass plates for special purposes. The photographic films available today are the result of much research and are very different from the earlier types. Every roll of film has at least five layers, as shown in the enlarged cross-section in the illustration on the right.

The first layer is known as the topcoat. It is a protective layer of hard gelatin which helps protect the emulsion from scratches or other foreign substances.

The second layer, the emulsion, usually contains light-sensitive silver bromide and silver iodide. These light-sensitive particles in the emulsion layer are made more so by the addition of certain sensitizing agents. Upon exposure to light and chemical development, the silver is reduced to fine particles of silver metal that look black.

The third layer, the subbing, is a glue-like substance that holds the emulsion layer to the base. In the past, many unusual materials were used for this purpose. One of the most popular subbing materials was egg white (albumen).

The fourth layer, the support or base of the film, is generally a plastic, usually a cellulose acetate. Its purpose is to provide a transparent and flexible foundation for the emulsion. At one time the support was made out of nitrocellulose, a highly flammable early plastic. Nitrocellulose was commonly used in early motion picture films, resulting in frequent fires.

The fifth and last layer is the antihalation backing. The purpose of this layer is to prevent light from reflecting off the support layer or the back of the camera itself during exposure. If these reflections were not eliminated, light areas on the film would have halos around them, which would reduce the sharpness of the image. The antihalation layer appears as the bluish or grayish color on one side of the film. Both the antihalation backing and the topcoat layers are dissolved away during processing.

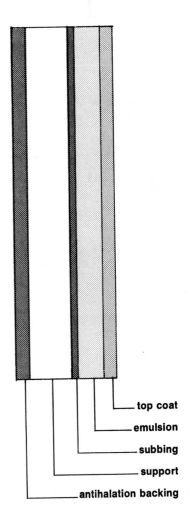

enlarged side view of film

top coat

emulsion

subbing

support

antihalation backing

Characteristics

Film has four characteristics: (1) color sensitivity, (2) speed (ASA), (3) grain, and (4) contrast. Black-and-white emulsions are classified into three groups in their ability to differentiate between colors—blue-sensitive, orthochromatic, and panchromatic. Blue-sensitive film uses the pure state of the silver bromide which makes the emulsion sensitive to light. Blue-sensitive film is sensitive to blue and ultraviolet light. It is high in contrast, which makes it useful for copying manuscripts, drawings, and other materials that do not have a long tonal range.

Orthochromatic film is sensitive to green light, as well as to blue and ultraviolet. However, orthochromatic film is not sensitive to red. If a red object such as a fire hydrant were shot with orthochromatic film, it would appear as a black tone in the photo. Be-

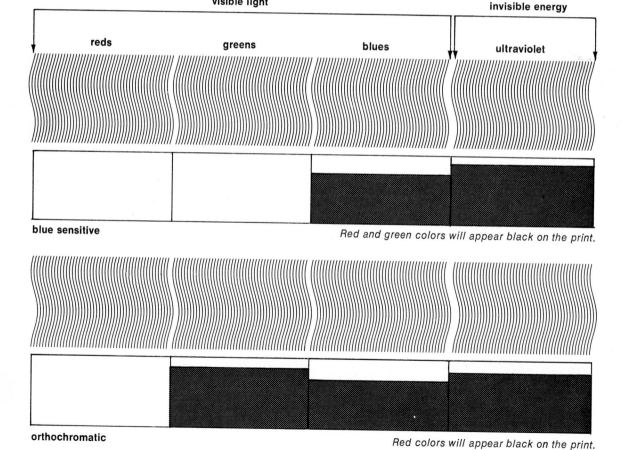

blue sensitive

Red and green colors will appear black on the print.

orthochromatic

Red colors will appear black on the print.

cause ortho emulsions are not sensitive to red, they can be handled in red safelight illumination. Most black and white photographic papers are orthochromatic.

Panchromatic film is sensitive to all the colors of the spectrum. Because it is sensitive to all colors, it gives the most natural-looking interpretation of color in terms of black and white tonal scale. In almost all cases, the films that you have been using are probably panchromatic. To summarize, panchromatic films are sensitive to all colors, orthochromatic films are sensitive to all but red, and blue-sensitive films are sensitive to only blue and violet light (plus radiation).

Speed, the second characteristic of film, is the sensitivity of film to light. Speed is measured on a scale set by the American Standards Association, referred to as the "ASA". The higher the speed, or ASA number, of the film, the more sensitive it is to light. The

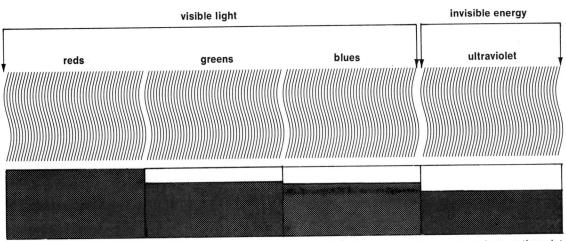

panchromatic

Red, green, and blue colors will appear in proportional gray values on the print.

These graphs are only approximate.

lower the ASA number, the less sensitive the film is to light. For example, the ASA of Kodak's Tri-X® is 400. The ASA of another Kodak film, Plus-X,® is 125. Therefore, Tri-X® is "faster" than Plus-X®: that is, it requires less light for exposure. The faster the film, the less light needed for exposure.

There is a definite correlation between the ASA rating numbers. Suppose we start with a base ASA of 25. ASA 50 would be twice

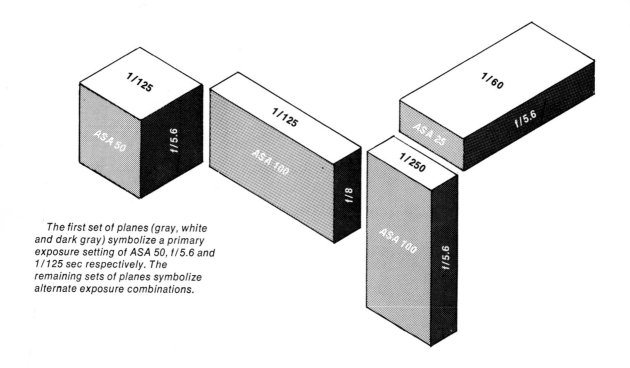

The first set of planes (gray, white and dark gray) symbolize a primary exposure setting of ASA 50, f/5.6 and 1/125 sec respectively. The remaining sets of planes symbolize alternate exposure combinations.

as fast as ASA 25. ASA 100 would be twice as fast as 50 and four times as fast as ASA 25. This is the same type of correlation that exists between shutter speeds, and f-stops. For example, given a certain lighting situation, let us presume that using an ASA 50 film at f/5.6 wth a shutter speed of 1/125 will produce a correct exposure. If an ASA of 100 instead of 50 were used, the correct exposure would be f/8 at 1/125 or f/5.6 at 1/250. In the case of the f-stop, you have to decrease the amount of light by one stop (half the amount of light) in order to get a correct exposure when the ASA is doubled. This, in turn, will increase the depth of field. In the case of the shutter speed, we have increased it by one speed; that is, we are allowing half as much light to pass through the lens. The result of this is that the subject will be frozen in action. Whenever a smaller lens opening is preferred for more depth of field, or a quicker shutter speed is desired to freeze action, a higher ASA film should be used.

"Grain," the third characteristic of film, refers to the bunching or clumping of the reduced silver portions in the emulsion during development. Grain exists in all photographs. A "grainy" print is one in which the clumping of the silver particles is very noticeable.

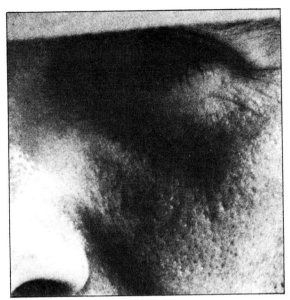

ASA 32 developed normally

ASA 800 developed normally

However, certain rules can be followed to control graininess. First, the higher the ASA of the film, the grainier it is. When image smoothness is essential, use a slower (lower ASA) film. Second, overexposure and overdevelopment contribute to graininess. Third, enlarging an image to a high magnification will cause grain to be seen more readily. This is why cropping is not recommended. A 5″ x 7″ print made from a 35mm negative looks very good. However, if that same negative were enlarged to 16″ x 20″ size, it might look like sandpaper. Fourth, graininess is also controlled by the type of film developer used. Some developers are made to be used with fine grain films, while others produce very harsh grain.

The fourth characteristic of film is contrast—the ability of the film to distinguish between the tones or values of gray. Some films are high in contrast and are used only to copy line drawings or manuscripts. Most films that you will be using can reproduce a wide tonal range.

Film also has other characteristics, such as latitude, acutance, and resolving power. The science of sensitometry is related to the study of film characteristics. If you are interested in this field, there are many fairly technical reference books on this subject.

Brands of Films

There are many different film manufacturers both in the United States and abroad. Because film is constantly being improved and changed, it is wise to check the information sheet packed with each individual roll to obtain the newest data about a film. The following is a list of the most popular black-and-white films manufactured by Eastman Kodak, along with descriptions of their characteristics.

Panatomic-X® (ASA 32). Panatomic can reproduce the greatest amount of detail and has the finest grain of any of the films listed here. However, it has a slow ASA, which limits its use in dim light.

Verichrome Pan® (ASA 125). Verichrome is a medium-speed film which is normally used in nonadjustable cameras. It has a medium fine grain.

Plus-X® (ASA 125). This is a medium fine grain film with a speed that is adequate for most picture-taking situations. Plus-X is the general, all-purpose film.

Tri-X® (ASA 400). This is a very fast film and so is useful for picture-taking in existing light indoors. It is also useful when depth of field and/or faster shutter speeds are needed. Tri-X, because of its high ASA, does not have as fine a grain as the other films in this listing.

Filters and Light

Although all panchromatic films are sensitive to every color in the spectrum, they are more sensitive to certain colors. Because of this, filters are used to lighten or darken objects of a particular color.

A filter is usually a colored piece of glass that is placed in front of the lens. Usually, it screws into the diameter of the lens. Like any filter, it absorbs what is not wanted and passes or transmits what is wanted. Understanding filters requires some knowledge of the behavior of light. Light is radiant energy that travels in waves. In visible light, the longest wave is red, the middle length, green, and the shortest violet. With those wavelength groups are the various hues of red, orange, yellow, green, and blue. If there are no waves, then there is no light. When all the waves travel together, the result is white light.

In a way, any object we see as having color is acting like a filter, because it is absorbing parts of the white light. The color we see is part of the light that is reflected back to us. For example, a red apple seems to be red because it absorbs blue and green light and reflects red light. (See Fig. 8-1.) Yellow paper looks yellow because it absorbs blue light and reflects both green and red. The table that follows lists certain types of color as they appear in white light and colors of light that are absorbed.

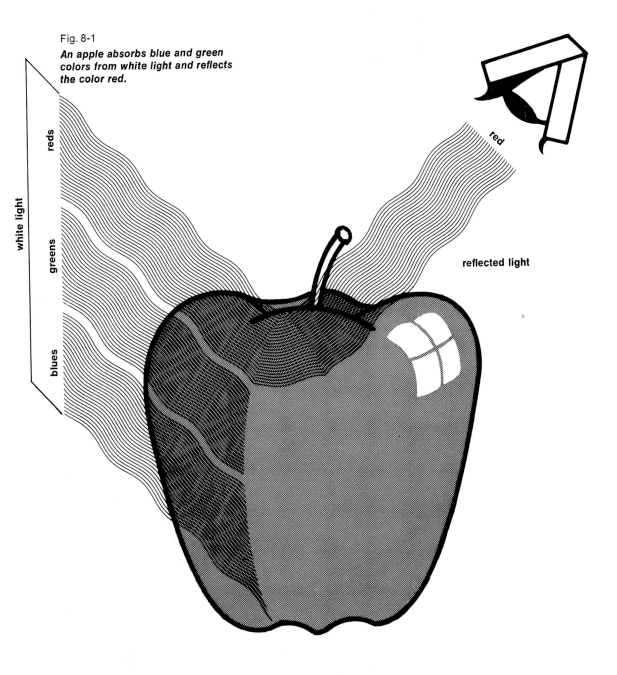

Fig. 8-1

An apple absorbs blue and green colors from white light and reflects the color red.

white light

reds

greens

blues

red

reflected light

Color seen in white light	Colors of light absorbed
red	blue-green
green	red and blue
blue	red and green
yellow (red plus green)	blue
magenta (red-blue)	green
cyan (blue-green)	red
black	red, green, blue
white	none
gray	equal portions of red, green, blue

Understanding filters is quite easy once you understand the principle that they always *subtract* some of the light from a scene. Remember that you are dealing with negative-positive relationships. When a filter absorbs a color, the area of that color will appear to be lighter in the negative. However, when the negative is printed, that color will appear darker.

Filters that are used for black-and-white pictures can be classified into three groups: (1) correction filters, (2) contrast filters, and (3) haze filters. Although panchromatic film is sensitive to all the colors of the spectrum, it is not sensitive to all of them equally. For instance, blue sky generally prints out to be very light in tone. To compensate, use a correction filter, which changes the tonal response of the film so that all colors are photographed at about the same brightness values as the eye originally saw. The most popular correction filter is a medium yellow (K-2). A photograph, taken with a yellow filter, reproduces the clouds as they were seen in their relative brightness values. They appear "bolder" because the blue sky appears darker. The yellow filter absorbed some blue light, thereby making blue appear darker in the print.

A contrast filter can either increase or decrease (lighten or darken) the contrast between colors. To make an object appear lighter than it is, use a filter that is the same color as the object. To make an object appear darker than it really is, use a filter that will absorb the color of the object. For example, compare these three black-and-white photographs of a red flower against green leaves. (See Fig. 8-2.) In the first photograph, no filter was used. Both the red and the green appear about the same tone of gray. In the second photograph, a red filter was used. A red filter transmits red light and absorbs green. Therefore, the red flower appears light while the color green, which was absorbed by the red filter, appears dark in the print. In the third photograph, a green filter was used. Green absorbs red light, thereby making the red flower appear darker than the green leaves. Keep in mind that a filter transmits its own color, making that color lighter. To make a color darker, use a filter that will absorb that color. Refer to the chart to help you select an appropriate filter.

Contrast filters are also used to darken the sky. The medium yellow (K-2) filter is used to reproduce the sky as your eye would see it if you saw things in black and white instead of color. The deep yellow (G) filter will make the sky seem even darker than it normally appears. For even more dramatic effects, a medium red (A or No. 25) filter can be used. A deep red filter (No. 29 or F) will make the sky almost black.

When you photograph landscapes in the distance or from high altitudes, the picture tends to lose a certain amount of detail. This is caused by the bluish atmospheric haze which is caused by very small particles of dust and water vapor. The haze scatters ultraviolet light to which film is very sensitive although the eye cannot see it. To reduce atmospheric haze when photographing, you can use haze filters to filter out some of the ultraviolet light. The amount of haze is decreased with the following filters: K-2 yellow (medium), G (deep yellow), A (medium red) and F (deep red).

One filter that can be used to eliminate both haze and reflections or glare is the polarizing filter. As light is reflected from nonmetallic surfaces, it is polarized. That is, the light vibrates in only one

Fig. 8-2

no filter *red filter* *green filter*

direction. The light from the sky is polarized because it is reflected from nonmetallic particles in the atmosphere. The polarized filter removes glare by stopping the path of the polarized light. The angle of the light source is important when using a polarizing filter. To get the maximum effect from such a filter, the angle at which you view the reflecting light must be equal to the angle at which the light strikes the reflecting surface. For instance, if the sun were at approximately a 60° angle from a scene, you would get maximum effect with the polarizing filter if you took the picture at a 60° angle.

Most polarizing filters are double-threaded. One thread screws into the camera, while the other one lets you rotate the filter. If the camera you are using is not a single-lens reflex or view camera, place the filter to your eye and rotate it until the desired effect is obtained. Note that a marking on the filter, usually a white dot, is used to indicate the position of the rotation. After the desired effect is produced, place the filter on the camera, making sure that the marking is in the same position. If you have a single-lens reflex camera, you can see the effect by looking through the viewfinder while you rotate the screen.

The polarizing filter is useful when photographing water, glass, or most other shiny surfaces. For example, these two photographs were taken through window glass. The first photo was taken without a polarizing filter thus, most of the subject is blocked out by the reflections or glare. In the second photograph, a polarizing filter was used. The reflections are eliminated, allowing more detail to be seen.

not polarized

polarized

Filter Factors

Because filters absorb some light, you must increase the exposure to compensate. The number by which you multiply the exposure is called the filter factor. If a filter has a factor of 2, you must either double your exposure time by decreasing your shutter speed by one speed or open the lens one stop. For example, a yellow filter has a factor of 2. If the proper reading without the filter were 1/250 at f/8, then with the filter it would be either 1/125 at f/8 or 1/250 at f/5.6. Generally, it is best to change the f-number rather than the shutter speed. If two filters are used together, the filter factors are added together. For example, the filter factor of a yellow (K-2) is 2. The filter factor of a polarizer is 2.5. If both are used together, your factor will be 5. You should then multiply your exposure time by 5 or increase your lens opening by 2⅓ f-stops.

Filter factors depend on the type of light and the film being used. The deep yellow (G) filter has a daylight factor of 2.5 with Kodak Plus-X® film. However, when you use artificial light (tungsten), like that from photofloods, the factor is 1.5. The reason for this is that sunlight contains more ultraviolet and blue light than photofloods give out. Therefore, outdoors in sunlight the deep yellow filter absorbs a greater portion of the light, and additional exposure is needed to compensate for this loss.

If your camera has a through-the-lens metering system, you do not have to worry about filter factors. This type of meter reads the light after it has already passed through the filter; the exposure reading is therefore based on the reduced amount of light.

Assignment: Film and Filters

1. Discuss the relationship of the speed (ASA), grain size, and contrast of the most commonly used films. Which of the above three film characteristics would be most important if you wanted to:
   a. photograph very fine detail. Why?
   b. take pictures indoors using normal room light. Why?
2. How much more sensitive to light is a film which is ASA 100 than a film which is ASA 25? Why? If you were shooting ASA 25 film with an f-stop of 5.6, what would be the equivalent f-stop in terms of exposure if you changed to ASA 100 film?
3. If you are shooting black and white film using a blue filter, what effect will the filter have upon blue colored objects:
   a. in your negative?
   b. in the positive (print) made from the negative? Why?
4. Why might you want to use a medium yellow filter when shooting outdoors?
5. What is a "filter factor"? If you were using a filter with a filter factor of 4, how many f-stops and in which direction would you have to move the f-stop ring in order to compensate for the filter factor?

Light

9

We are able to see because of the presence of light. The more light available, the brighter an object appears. Without light, we are blind. Light also makes photography possible. When light is recorded on film, an image forms. Whether that image is abstract or realistic depends on the photographer's control of light. By controlling that light, he or she is free to determine expression and impressions in a scene. You, as a photographer, can use light to communicate atmosphere and mood. You can establish an interrelationship of patterns and forms within the boundaries of a photograph. You can begin to realize the full potential of the art of photography.

Existing Light Photography

Light can be added to a scene with the use of artificial light sources such as photo flash, electronic flash, or floodlights. However, once light is added to a subject, the picture no longer possesses one of the inherent qualities of photography—the capturing of an unplanned moment. Existing light photography—picture-taking in available light—allows the photographer an endless array of photographic possibilities. They range from a photograph taken with a single candle as illumination to a brilliantly sunlit view of the Grand Canyon. The term "existing light," however, has come to mean pictures taken in low light levels. Usually these are indoor scenes with a variety of light sources, such as candles, lightbulbs, window light and stage lighting like that at rock concerts. Picture-taking in available light requires certain equipment. The camera lens should be reasonably fast, at least f/2.8 or faster. If a slower lens were used, the necessary shutter speed required for a correct exposure would be so long that the picture would be blurred. For the same reason, the film should also be fast, ASA 400 or better. Two other equipment items should be considered for existing light photography, especially for very dimly illuminated subjects such as night scenes. These are a tripod and a cable release. When you are taking pictures at shutter speeds slower than 1/30, any movement of the camera will cause blurry images. Since you cannot hold perfectly still this long, you use the tripod to support the camera as you shoot. Assuming that the tripod is on a solid, vibration-free surface, you can eliminate such vibrations. A cable release is a flexible cord that enables the photographer to trip the shutter button as the camera rests on the tripod. Some cable releases have locks that, with the camera on the "B" setting, will keep the shutter open as long as the photographer wishes.

Exposure Considerations

Illumination in existing light photography is unfortunately often very contrasty. For example, the light around the bulb of a street light is very bright, a few feet away that illumination stops and total darkness begins. Because of this, exposure literally becomes "a shot in the dark."

You will often want to use existing light for pictures of people. However, you may find yourself in light so low that your exposure meter doesn't seem to work. In that case, use a white card for your reading, rather than the person's face. The correct exposure will be about 2½ times the exposure indicated on the card. For example, at a shutter speed of 1/60 you might get a reading of f/8 off the white card. You would then open your lens 1½ f-stops to a setting halfway between f/4 and f/2.8. However, it is still preferable to take your reading directly off the subject's face.

Another situation in which you want to use existing light is in photographing concerts or plays. Although the stage lights are often very bright, they are directed at only a few people, while the rest of the stage is dark. It is important to avoid the dark areas on the stage when calculating exposure. You will tend to overexpose such pictures because the dark areas combined with the spotlight areas tell the meter that there is less light on the stage than actually exists. Be sure that you always expose only the area in the spotlight. It is best, if possible, to walk up to the stage and take a meter reading off your hand. Use that meter reading no matter where you are sitting when you actually shoot the picture. However, if this is impossible, point the meter toward the stage from where you are seated and then close the lens down by at least one f-stop. Remember, that meter reading takes into account the dark areas and so is based in part upon a lack of light, while actually there is a great deal of light on stage.

The best thing to do with existing light is bracketing the exposure. In other words, if the correct exposure is 1/30 at f/5.6, take another picture at 1/30 at f/8 and one more at 1/30 at f/4. This should allow for any error in your judgment of the exposure.

Because existing light photography requires a film with a high ASA number, grain may be a problem. To minimize this, try not to overexpose your negatives. Overexposure coupled with a high

Use a cable release for slow shutter speeds

ASA film will result in large clumps of grain in the photo, making the image less sharp.

Shutter speeds for existing light photography are generally slow. When possible, use a tripod and cable release. If your subjects move during a slow exposure time, the image will blur. Some subject movement can add interesting effects to a photograph. Camera movement, though, usually ruins the picture.

Existing light photography usually requires that the *f*-stop be wide open, and so depth of field is not very great. You must focus the shot very carefully. (It is best to focus on the eyes when photographing people.)

Existing light photography offers many photographic possibilities, for pictures taken in natural light look honest and candid. However, there are many times when existing light photography is just not possible or acceptable. Sometimes there is not enough light for a picture; some subjects cannot be seen to their best advantage in existing light. Whatever the reasons, you also need to know how to use artificial light sources.

Artificial Light Sources

Artificial light sources for photography are of two kinds: instantaneous and continuous. Instantaneous light sources include all the varieties of flashbulbs, and electronic flash. Continuous light sources are photo floodlights, spotlights, or any other light that remains on after the exposure has been made. Flashbulbs, probably the most popular light source, are a fairly recent development. Before their invention, flash powder was used. It was a compound of chemicals that, when ignited, produced a bright flash and clouds

109

flash cube

of smoke. It often caused burned hands, singed hair, and occasionally a good house fire. Flash powder is seldom used today except by a few nostalgic photographers who long for the good old days.

A flashbulb is a glass bulb filled with shredded foil of hydroaluminum in an oxidizing atmosphere. Electricity passes through a filament encased in a primer which ignites the shredded foil and causes a flash of light. Flashbulbs differ in the amount of light they can give off, the amount of time they emit light, the color of the light, and its direction. Popular bulbs include these (starting with the least powerful): AG1 or AG1B (B means blue), M2 or M2B, M3 or M3B, 5 or 5B, 6 or 6B. Each of these bulbs needs a reflector to direct the light. The smaller the reflector, the more concentrated the light; the larger the reflector, the more area the light will cover. The type of reflector used with each of these bulbs is one of the elements that determine exposure.

Another type of flashbulb is the flash cube. There are two types of flash cubes, the regular cube (also known as Supercubes®) and X cubes (also known as Magicubes®). The regular cubes are powered by batteries in the camera, while the X cube is set off mechanically. Both types of cubes contain integral reflectors and will give four separate flashes per cube. Most Instamatic-type cameras are equipped with a socket to hold either a magic cube or a regular cube. A new General Electric bulb, called Flip-Flash® will yield 8 separate flashes.

The more popular instantaneous light source is the electronic flash. It may consist of a battery (sometimes rechargeable), a capacitor, and a flash tube. The battery sends electricity into the capacitor, where it is stored. When the energy is released, it produces a bright, split-second flash in the flash tube. The flash tube, unlike the flashbulb, is reusable for many thousands of flashes. Because of this, electronic flash has become increasingly popular. It can be adapted for most types of cameras. Some electronic flash units are more powerful than others. These produce more light and allow the photographer to take pictures at a greater distance or with a smaller lens opening. Other variables in electronic flash units are rechargeable batteries, AC power supplies, and the angle of the flash.

Flash Exposure

Flash exposure is simplified by using guide numbers. A guide number represents an *f*-number multiplied by the distance of the subject. The manufacturer of the light source assigns a guide number for any combination of film speed, type of flash (size), and reflector. These are found on any package of flashbulbs or in the instruction manual of an electronic flash. Suppose you were using an ASA 64 film and a shutter speed of 1/30 with a regular flash cube. The guide number for this combination is 80. To find the correct lens opening, divide the distance from flash source to subject into 80. For example, if your subject is 10 feet away, divide 80 by 10 (= 8). For this picture, f/8 at 1/30 would yield a correct exposure.

Another example of how guide numbers work: Suppose you were using a faster ASA film such as Plus-X® (ASA 125) with AG1B flashbulbs. In this case, a reflector must be used on the flash or the light will be scattered. A larger reflector will decrease the guide number, while a smaller reflector which concentrates the light more will increase it. The reflector for this example is small, so the guide number is 160. The flash-to-subject distance remains at 10 feet. By dividing 10 into 160 we get 16. The correct exposure is 1/30 at f/16 at a distance of 10 feet.

electronic flash

Guide numbers for flashbulbs are usually based on a shutter speed of 1/30. For electronic flash, the shutter speed is usually irrelevant to the guide number. It is important that the flash be synchronized with the shutter; that is, it should peak while the shutter is fully open. Otherwise, only part of the photograph will be illuminated by the light, while the remaining part is dark.

Different types of flash are synchronized for different shutter speeds on various cameras, for example, Class M, FP, and X.

Class M bulbs are medium-peak. In other words, they reach their full brilliance after the shutter button is released. Cameras equipped with M synchronization incorporate a delaying device that gives the flashbulb a headstart before the shutter opens. By the time the shutter is fully opened (about 20 milliseconds after the shutter button is released), the lamp and the shutter are in full synchronization.

Class FP lamps are used for cameras that have a focal plane shutter (such as most single-lens reflex cameras). FP lamps like 6226 can peak for 40 milliseconds. The "peak" must be this long because the focal plane shutter has a slit in the curtain that passes across the film, exposing it to the light. Therefore, the bulb has to peak longer to compensate for the time it takes for the whole curtain to travel across the film.

Type X synchronization is used for electronic flash. Here the flash peaks very fast. When the shutter button is depressed, and before the shutter is fully opened, the flash must be reaching its peak. If the peak occurs after or before the shutter is fully opened, part of the picture will be dark. Shutter speed selection for X synchronization will depend upon the type of shutter in your camera. If the camera is equipped with a focal plane shutter, the speed is usually synchronized at 1/60. The focal plane shutter travels horizontally (sideways) across the film. Some cameras have metal "Copal" shutters, which travel up and down instead of sideways. These shutters are synchronized at 1/125. If the camera has a between-the-lens shutter, then speed selection usually doesn't matter. Check your camera instruction manual to find what speed should be used for X synchronization.

Many flash units today, especially electronic ones, are equipped with dials that automatically calculate exposure without the need of guide numbers. In the illustration, notice that the ASA indicator is pointing at 100. The distance scale is marked off in feet. If the flash-to-subject distance is 10 feet, the number above 10 is 8. The f-stop is, therefore, f/8. If the flash-to-subject distance is 15 feet, then, according to the dial, the f-stop would be f/4. Such dials of this type facilitate calculating exposures.

Many manufacturers of electronic flash units unfortunately assign a guide number that is too high. In this case, you will constantly have underexposed negatives. Should this happen, you may want to use a larger lens opening than the one recommended by the flash unit (probably one-half to one full stop). This adjustment will require some testing. However, once you know how much to open your lens, it becomes a matter of routine since the amount of light doesn't vary from flash to flash.

Using Flash

Flashbulbs or electronic flash can usually be used in the same ways as natural or artificial light. Flash units are most commonly attached to the camera, giving you the advantages of both speed and convenience. You need not hold or aim the flash separately. This is convenient when photographing action, such as sports events. Calculating exposure is usually more accurate because the camera and flash are the same distance from the subject. However, there are some disadvantages to having the flash attached to the camera. The major one is that the picture may have a washed-out background and probably a harsh shadow behind the subject. (See Fig. 9-1.) Another disadvantage is that the subject will have little or no modeling. For an object to look three-dimensional, there must be both shadows and highlights. A camera-mounted flash usually makes people's faces look flat. One way to avoid this is to keep the flash above and slightly to one side of the subject. Remove the flash unit from the camera and either attach it to an "L" bracket (See Fig. 9-2) or hold it in your free hand. However, it is difficult to hold the camera steady when using only one hand.

Bouncing the light is another way to soften it. (See Fig. 9-3.) This is done by aiming the flash at a surface that will reflect the light back onto the subject, such as white walls and ceilings or mirrors. Bounce light, however, reduces the amount of light on your subject, and so you must increase the exposure. A quick rule of thumb is to open the lens two stops. A more accurate way is to measure the flash to the reflecting surface and from the surface to the subject. Divide the total into the guide number to determine exposure. Remember that bounce light only works in a small, light area and that dark colors absorb light while light colors reflect it.

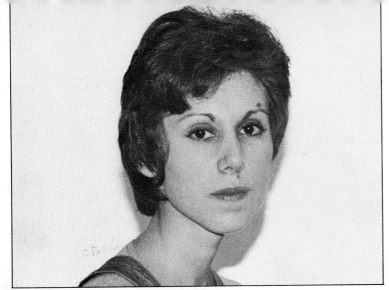

Fig. 9-1
flash on camera

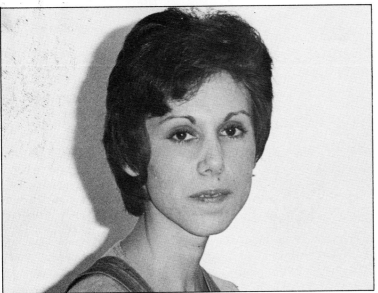

Fig. 9-2
flash off camera

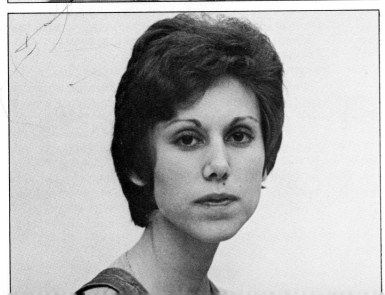

Fig. 9-3
flash bounced off ceiling or wall

no fill

normal fill

bright fill

Using Flash Outdoors

When photographing portraits outdoors, you will probably want to "fill in" the deep shadows under the eyes that bright sunlight creates. To do this, you will need a long PC cord (the cord which plugs into the camera from the flash). First, calculate the exposure of the subject as if you were not using the flash at all. After the exposure is known, divide the flash guide number by the f-stop you have selected. This will give you the flash-to-subject distance. Remember that some cameras are synchronized for flash at a certain shutter speed only. Most SLRs are synchronized at 1/60 with electronic flash. So, you will have to calculate the exposure at 1/60 if you are planning to add electronic flash. For a "bright fill," place your flash at this distance. For example, suppose your exposure was 1/60 at f/8 with an ASA 25 film. The guide number of the flash was 40, so you would divide 8 into 40 and place your flash 5 feet from your subject. Unless you want to take the picture from 5 feet, it may be necessary to use a support like a tripod to hold the flash. Be sure to direct the flash at the subject.

"Bright fill" will wash out all shadow detail in your subject's face. For a "normal fill," move the flash back half again the distance. In the example given above, you would move it 2½ feet more, for a total of 7½ feet. Normal fill allows some darkening under the eyes. For still more darkening or shadow area, "weak fill" can be used. This allows almost as much shadow under the eyes and mouth as there would have been without the flash. For weak fill, double the bright fill distance. Using the same example, you would place the flash 10 feet away—double the distance for bright fill.

Continuous Light Sources

Continuous light sources are any light that provides a steady flow of artificial illumination. A flashlight, for instance, gives a steady flow of light, although it is not normally bright enough for photography. Certain types of lightbulbs have been designed for photographic purposes. Called photofloods, they provide an even, steady flow of light that is bright enough for photographing. The light from photoflood bulbs must be directed. This can be done with either reflectors or reflector floods. (See Fig. 9-4.) Reflectors direct the light so that it travels at a certain angle. Generally, the larger the reflector, the more area the light will cover. Usually the smaller the reflector, the more concentrated the light will be. A large reflector with a 12-inch radius, for instance, would be used to light a large area such as a room. Reflector floodlights are photo flood bulbs with built-in reflectors. This type of light source provides a concentrated light beam. Reflector floods are useful when the light is to be directed on a small area, like the face. Both types of bulbs must be mounted in a light socket. A clamp and cord set provide a socket as well as a clamp to fasten the unit on a chair or other support. The bulb can also be fastened on an adjustable light stand, which can be lowered and raised like a camera tripod.

Reflectors and bulbs give you an effective way to control light. A typical lighting set-up in a professional studio may use as many as seven different lights at different angles. These give a more even light than found in daylight. However, many successful portraits can be done using one to three lights.

Try this exercise to practice different lighting techniques. Use a Number 2 photoflood lamp, which uses 500 watts of light (a Number 1 lamp uses 250 watts). Attach the bulb to a clamp or light stand with an 8"-12" reflector. (You can also use a reflector flood alone.) Either ask a friend to model or place a mannequin head (with painted features) in front of a white wall or screen. Set the camera about 3 to 5 feet from the head. The image of the head should fill the viewfinder. This distance should not vary with each photograph. There should be no lights in the room except the photo lamp. *Shot #1*—place the light as near the camera as possible, aimed squarely at the subject. *Shot #2*—place the light on the left side of the subject at a 45° angle to the camera-subject line. *Shot #3*—same position as #2 but raise the light to shine down on the subject at a 20° angle. *Shot #4*—same position, but lower the light to beam up at the subject. *Shot #5*—place the light so that it beams directly down on the subject's forehead. *Shot #6* —place the light directly below the subject's face, aiming up toward the chin. *Shot #7*—aim the light behind the subject onto the white background.

After the photos have been developed and printed, compare them. The first photo will show the subject well lighted without shadows. However, the features will appear flat. Shot #2 will be a contrasty rendering of the subject, with deep shadows beside the nose and mouth. Shot #3 will show the subject with deep shadows under both eyes and underneath the mouth. In Shot #4, the face

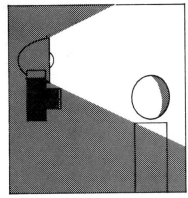

1. light source near camera

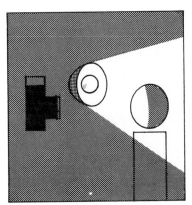

2. 45° to the left

3. same as 2 but 20° higher

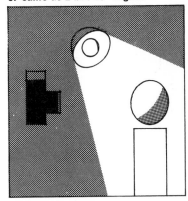

Fig. 9-4

photoflood lamp with reflector

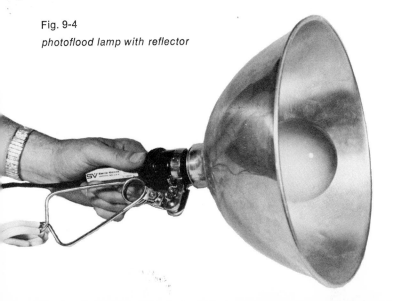

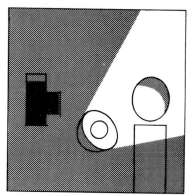

4. same as 2 but 20° lower

will look somewhat strange because the shadows fall upward. Shot #5 will have extreme shadows under the eyes and mouth. Shot #6 will make the subject look scary and grotesque. Shot #7 produces a silhouette.

After you have done this exercise, you may want to experiment with more lights. For a two-light combination, keep the camera-to-subject distance the same. Shoot seven pictures of the subject in the same sequence as above. The only change will be the addition of a Number 1 flood light (250 watts) on the right at a 45° angle from the subject and camera line. How will the second light change the picture? A third light, aimed from well above and a little behind the subject, will add texture to the hair. The third light should not be bright, since you only want to highlight the hair.

Exposure Calculations

When reading the meter for a subject illuminated by artificial light, it is usually best to average several readings together. (See Chapter 3.) In other words, take an exposure reading from various areas of the subject, such as hair, face, clothes, and shadow areas, and then find the average exposure. If the subject is to be silhouetted on purpose, then read the background area only.

One physical law about the behavior of light is important to know when using artificial light: The intensity of light falls off rapidly as the distance between the light source and subject is increased. In mathematical terms, the illumination of a surface is inversely proportional to the square of the distance between the light source and the illuminated surface. If you double the distance between the subject and the light source, the light becomes only one-fourth as bright. For example, if the correct reading were 1/125 at f/11 with the light 10 feet from the subject, moving the light back

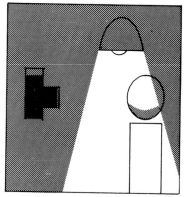

5. straight down

6. straight up

7. light on background

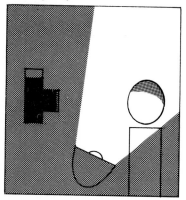

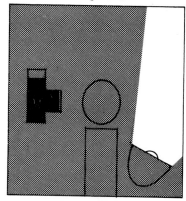

116

to 20 feet (twice the distance) would mean the exposure should be increased to 1/125 at 5.6. The closer the light is to the subject, the more light the subject will reflect, thus requiring a shorter exposure time. The longer the distance between the subject and light source, the less intense the light will be. Less light will be reflected, and the exposure will have to be longer.

Whatever kind of light you choose for your photograph, artificial or natural, learn to control it to achieve what you want.

Assignment: Light

1. What is meant by "existing light" photography? What things should you keep in mind when shooting in existing light, that is, what film is best, what type of lens, what will be some common problems in shooting in existing light?
2. What are some disadvantages to using a single source of light mounted on a camera, such as a flashbulb or an electronic flash unit?
3. What effect does "bounce lighting" have on your photograph? How do you calculate exposure when using bounce lighting?
4. Shoot two series of photographs with at least 3 photographs in each series. One series should use a person's face as its subject, the second series should use an object or collection of objects as the subject. The two series should illustrate how the same subject can appear different and communicate a different mood as the lighting is changed. All the light used in these photographs should be directly controlled by you through the use of artificial light sources.

10 feet   20 feet

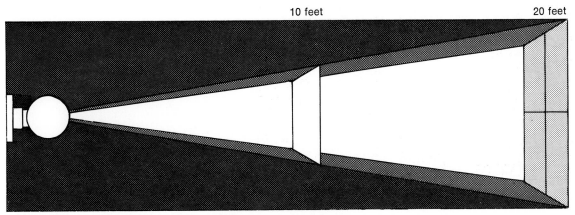

Light incidence is four times more intense at 10 feet than at 20 feet.

Lenses

The purpose of a lens is to gather light and to direct that light to the film. The pinhole camera, which had no lens, produced images that were not sharp and had little contrast between tones. A lens provides a definite plane of focus, giving a sharp, focused image and increasing the contrast between tones. A photographer need not know everything about lens design or construction in order to take a good photograph. However, the more you know about how lenses work, the better your chances are of taking that good photograph.

Lens design is based on the principle that light is bent, or refracted, as it passes from air to glass or glass to air, as it does in a prism. In the case of a double prism, a second ray of light begins at the same point. It enters the lower prism and is eventually bent back upward so that they both meet at a common point. Lenses are made in different shapes and sizes, but can be classified as negative or positive based on how they disperse light rays. In a negative lens, the light rays diverge or spread out as they pass through the lens. In a positive lens, the light rays converge at a common point. More sophisticated lenses contain not one piece of glass but many. In these lenses, each piece of glass is called an element. The various shapes and combinations of elements (called groupings) determine the quality and use of a particular lens.

Terminology

Understanding lenses requires your knowing some of the technical terms used in describing them:

Focal point. All rays of light approach a lens from a point of infinity. These rays of light are parallel as they travel through air until they enter a lens. After they are bent by the lens, they converge at a common point, the *focal point.* More specifically, the focal point is the point where the light rays converge when the lens is focused at infinity. Basically a thin lens causes light rays to converge at a farther point than a thick lens. Consequently, the film in the camera is placed at the focal point of the lens. This area of the

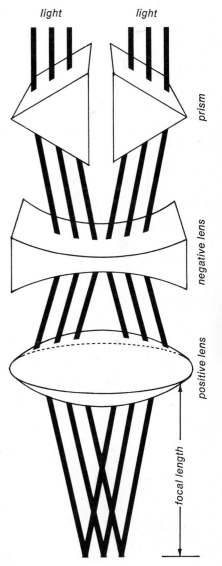

light   light

prism

negative lens

positive lens

focal length

camera is called the focal plane.

Circles of confusion. If you recall from Chapter 2, the Pinhole Camera, the larger the hole size was, the fuzzier the image became. The smaller the hole, the sharper the image was. This is due to an optical effect called "circles of confusion."

Examine the following illustration. (See Fig. 10-1.) Figure A represents the subject that is being photographed. B represents the pinhole. C represents how the image will be recorded on the film. Notice that the image is upside down and reversed and is made up of tiny little circles. Only a few rays of light from each point on the subject can pass through the small opening. These "light rays" strike the film in very tight clusters so that blurring is reduced to a minimum.

The size of the opening was increased in this second illustration. (See Fig. 10-2.) The larger hole allows a greater number of rays from each point on the subject to enter the camera. These light rays spread before reaching the film and are recorded as large circles. Because of their size, these circles overlap each other, thus creating a blurry photograph. In other words, the larger the circles are, the more they will overlap and the blurrier the

small pinhole projects light clusters

Fig. 10-1

subject

pinhole

projected image

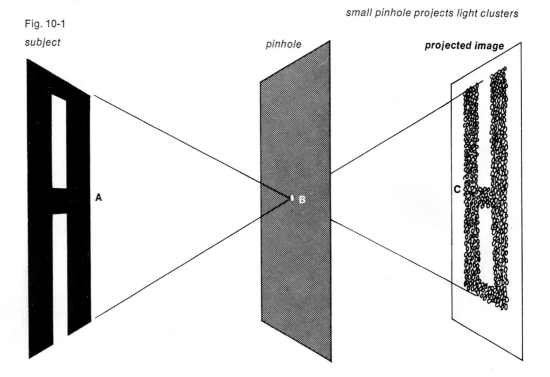

picture will be. These circles, which make up all photographic images, are called circles of confusion.

Focal length. The focal length of a lens is a factor that determines the size of the image on the film, the picture angle covering the area of the subject to be photographed, the brightness of the image, the depth of field, and the *f*-stop. Focal length is the optical distance from the lens, when focused at infinity (not necessarily the middle of the lens), to the focal point. In Chapter 2, you learned about pinhole-to-film distance in the pinhole camera. Had there been a lens on the pinhole, this distance could have been called the focal length.

The focal length of a lens never changes, even if the lens is removed from the camera or if it is focused at a closer point than infinity. It is the result of the fundamental design of the lens.

f-number. Because of the variety of lenses available, a formula is used to describe the ability of a lens to gather light: f-N = FL/D. F-N represents the *f*-number, the maximum light-gathering ability of a lens. D represents the diameter of the lens. FL represents the focal length of the lens. (See Fig. 10-3.) The *f*-number, as you already know, is a fraction. It represents how many times the full

larger pinhole projects larger overlapping clusters

Fig. 10-2

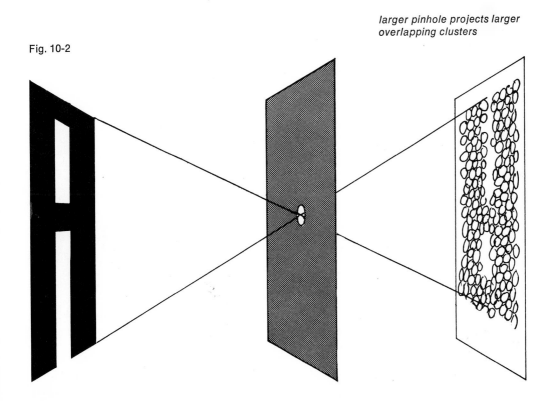

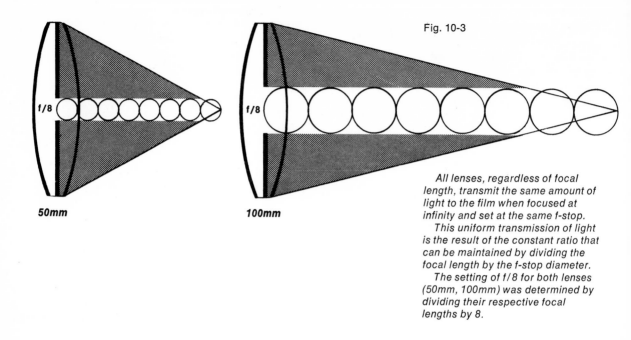

Fig. 10-3

All lenses, regardless of focal length, transmit the same amount of light to the film when focused at infinity and set at the same f-stop.

This uniform transmission of light is the result of the constant ratio that can be maintained by dividing the focal length by the f-stop diameter.

The setting of f/8 for both lenses (50mm, 100mm) was determined by dividing their respective focal lengths by 8.

50mm

100mm

effective diameter of the lens can be divided by the focal length. For example, if *f/8* is the widest opening on a lens, then the widest diameter of that lens is ⅛ the focal length. Because an *f*-number is based on the relationship of focal length and diameter, *f/8* on a lens with a 12-inch focal length allows just as much light to reach the film as *f/8* on a 6-inch focal length lens although the actual size of the opening will be different.

Depth of field. Depth of field (discussed in Chapter 3) is the range of distance, before and behind the subject, that is in acceptable focus. Among the factors that determine the depth of field are: (1) lens aperture, (2) focal length, and (3) focus distance.

The smaller the lens aperture, the greater the depth of field. The larger the lens opening, the smaller the depth of field. This is because a large opening produces larger circles of confusion while a small opening produces smaller circles of confusion.

Depth of field is influenced not only by aperture size but by the distance from camera to subject as well. The simple rule is, the closer you are to the subject you are focusing on, the fuzzier everything else will be, or the less your depth of field will be.

Another factor that affects depth of field is the focal length of the lens. A short focal length lens (wide-angle) has great depth of

graphic approximation of area in focus

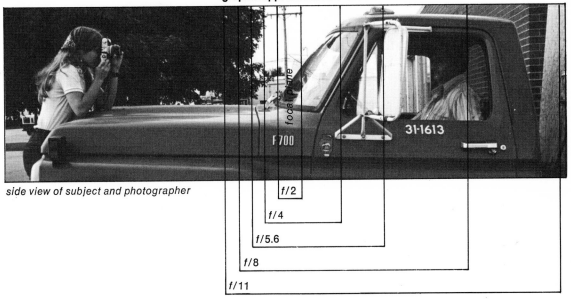

side view of subject and photographer

f/2
f/4
f/5.6
f/8
f/11

Fig. 10-4

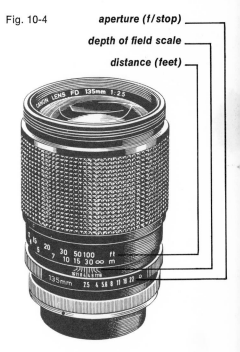

aperture (f/stop)
depth of field scale
distance (feet)

field at a given f-stop. The normal focal length lens has a longer focal length than the wide-angle, so depth of field is not as great. The telephoto lens, which has an even longer focal length, has very little depth of field. To summarize: The shorter the focal length, the greater the depth of field. The longer the focal length, the less depth of field.

Depth of field scales. The way in which depth of field is indicated on a camera depends on how the camera is focused. If the camera cannot be focused, its depth of field is fixed. Usually such cameras have great depth of field, giving acceptable sharpness between 6 feet and infinity. Other cameras have depth of field scales. On most single-lens reflex cameras, the depth of field scale is on the lens. (See Fig. 10-4.) To use this scale, first focus the lens at, say, 10 feet. Below the footage indicator is the depth of field scale, a double series of numbers representing f-numbers. To find the depth of field at a given f-stop, f/16 for example, read the distance scale at the points opposite the engraved "16" on both sides of the dot. (That dot is the reference marking for the distance.) You will see that the depth of field is from 6 feet (left of the dot) to 15 feet (right of the dot). Now suppose that you are using f/4 instead of f/16, while keeping the distance at 10 feet. Locating "4" on the left side of the dot, you find that the depth starts at 9 feet. To the right of the dot, depth of field ends at 12 feet. So the depth of field is less because the aperture size was increased.

Depth of field scales vary from camera to camera. It is always wise to check the instruction manual of your camera.

These scales do not give you any way of seeing depth of field. However, some cameras provide a depth-of-field preview button. Pressing this button will stop down the lens to a predetermined f-stop. You can see in the viewfinder what will be in focus and what will not.

Zone Focus

Zone focus is useful when photographing fast-moving subjects at sports events, etc. Because it is difficult to focus and refocus constantly, the camera is set for the distance where the subject is most likely to be. The depth of field scale or preview is then checked to see how far the subject can move without getting out of focus. As long as the subject remains within this range, pictures can be taken without refocusing.

Normal Focal Length Lenses

A normal lens and the human eye "see" objects the same size from the same distance. A "normal" lens for a 35mm camera is 50mm. An 80mm, focal length lens is considered normal for a 2¼" x 2¼" camera. For a particular camera, normal focal length lens is the diagonal measurement of the film. For instance, the diagonal measurement of 35mm film is almost 43mm. Thus, the normal focal length lens for 35mm is 50mm.

One thing to keep in mind is that a "normal" focal length lens for one camera using a certain size of film will not be normal for a different camera using a larger or smaller film size. For instance, a 50mm focal length is normal for 35mm film, but a 50mm lens used on 2¼" x 2¼" size film would be a "wide-angle."

The normal lens, which can usually be focused down to 2 feet, is the most popular focal length of a camera. Usually, the faster lens available with any camera is a normal lens. In other words, they can have an f-stop range up to f/2, making them very useful for existing light photography. However, there are times when you need a lens with a shorter or longer focal length—a wide-angle or telephoto. Of course, to use either a telephoto or wide-angle lens, you must have a camera on which you can substitute these lenses for the normal lens (called "lens interchangeability").

Telephoto Lenses

Sometimes your subject is too far away to be seen in a viewfinder. Sometimes you don't want the subject to know you are taking a picture. A telephoto lens, like a telescope, magnifies the subject so that it appears closer than it really is. Telephoto lenses are long focal length lenses. In other words, the focal length is longer than the diagonal measurement of the film. The longer the focal length, the larger the image on the film. As with normal lenses, a telephoto lens is relative to a particular size film.

Because there are so many telephoto lenses available, we will discuss only those used on 35mm cameras. One reason is that many more 35mm cameras are made with lens interchangeability.

85mm

Telephoto lenses for 35mm cameras are generally divided into three types—short, medium, or long. Short telephoto lenses are between 85mm and 105mm. Though small, they increase the image size recorded on the film. Many photographers use a short telephoto lens both for shooting subjects at a distance and for portrait work. The telephoto has two advantages for portrait work: (1) The camera can be placed farther from the subject's face, allowing a more relaxed, natural pose; and (2) a telephoto distorts facial features less than a normal lens used at minimum focus.

Medium focal length telephoto lenses are in the 135mm—200mm range. These middle-range lenses are probably the most popular telephotos. The 135mm lens can be used for portraits, sports events, and landscapes. They are also quite widely used for candid photographs of people. While a 100mm lens will double the image size on the negative, a 200mm lens will magnify the image four times.

135mm

Any lens longer than 200mm is usually classified as a long telephoto. These are used when the distance between photographer and subject is great—at a football game or ski run, for instance. They are also quite useful for photographing animals in their natural habitats. A 400mm lens will magnify the subject by 8. That is, if the subject were 80 feet away, it would appear to be only 10 feet away in the film image. One problem, however, is that perspective may be distorted.

200mm

Perspective is the relationship between objects in terms of position and distance, as seen from a certain viewpoint. A long focal length lens tends to compress or shorten the apparent distances between objects. A photo taken with a long telephoto lens looks flat and lacks depth. Because long lenses tend to "compress" objects, they are seldom used for portraiture. However, they are useful tools in many picture-taking situations.

125

When using any telephoto lens, remember that the longer the focal length, the less the depth of field. Telephoto lenses are usually heavier than other lenses and they generally are rather slow. Very few telephotos are faster than *f*/4. Because of the weight and the loss of depth of field, a fast shutter speed should be used. A tripod will provide good support for the camera with a long, heavy telephoto lens, especially if the focal length exceeds 200mm.

Wide-Angle Lenses

Wide-angle, or short focal length lenses are the opposite of the telephotos. They allow the photographer to record more of the total area of scene without moving the camera back. For example, if you had to be 20 feet away to photograph an object with a camera with a normal lens, using a wide-angle might allow you to shoot the same area from only 10 feet away.

The term "wide-angle" refers to the "angle of acceptance," the area "seen" by the lens. How wide this angle is depends on the

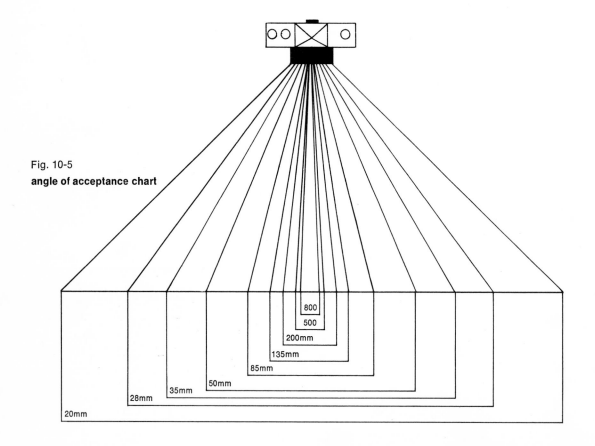

Fig. 10-5

angle of acceptance chart

800
500
200mm
135mm
85mm
50mm
35mm
28mm
20mm

focal length. Wide-angle lenses have short focal lengths. They are shorter than the diagonal measurement of the film. The shorter the focal length, the wider the angle of acceptance. For example a normal 50mm lens for a 35mm camera has an angle of acceptance of 46°. A 500mm telephoto for a 35mm camera has an angle of acceptance of only 5°. Clearly, the 500mm lens has a much narrower angle of acceptance, or angle of view. A 28mm wide-angle lens for a 35mm camera, however, has an angle of acceptance of 74°. A much wider area is covered. The chart illustrates these relationships (See Fig. 10-5). The focal lengths 20mm, 28mm, and 35mm are wide-angle lenses for 35mm film. The 50mm and 55mm are normal focal length lenses. In the telephotos, 85mm and 105mm are short, while 135mm and 200mm are medium telephotos. Beyond 200mm are the long focal length lenses. Starting with the 20mm wide-angle lens, notice how the angle of acceptance gets narrower. The diagram illustrates the differences in area covered by a wide-angle, a telephoto, and a normal lens for a 35mm camera.

The wide-angle lens also distorts perspective, but quite differently than a telephoto. Rather than compressing space, it exaggerates it. The shorter the focal length, the more it exaggerates space. For instance, if two objects are 10 feet apart, a wide-angle may make them look 15 or 20 feet apart. Because extreme wide-angle lenses make objects look circular, they are generally not used for portraits unless a special effect is wanted.

close-up with a wide-angle lens

The background is progressively condensed with each longer focal length lens.

wide angle

normal

telephoto

Zoom lens

Macro lens

Lens Systems

The 35mm single-lens reflex camera is ideally suited for using interchangeable lenses. It allows the photographer to look through the lens and see what effect each type of lens has on the photograph.

However, not all single-lens reflex cameras permit lens interchangeability. Check your camera instruction manual to determine whether the lens system is interchangeable and if so, the method for removing the lens. Some camera lenses simply screw off and another lens is screwed on. Some manufacturers use a bayonet system to lock the lens on the camera. A button is depressed to unlock the lens hinge, and the lens is then bayoneted or twisted off.

The use of different focal length lenses allows the photographer to choose from the many ways of expressing a thought or idea in a photograph.

Special Lenses

Many camera lens manufacturers produce an array of lenses for special purposes. These include fisheye, perspective control, macro, and zoom lenses. The fisheye is an extreme wide-angle lens which usually produces a circular image on the film. Some fisheye lenses are even capable of photographing objects slightly behind the lens because they are a 220° field of view. Generally they are used for scientific purposes, such as photographing cloud formations for weather records. However, fisheyes can also be used to achieve special effects.

Usually, when a camera is tilted upward, as in shooting a tall building, the sides appear to converge at the top. In other words, the building may look more like a pyramid than a rectangular structure. A perspective control lens (PC) can correct for this type of distortion because the lens, not the camera level, is raised. PC lenses are used in architectural work when a realistic interpretation is required.

Macro lenses are useful for most types of photography. They are normal lenses that can focus very close to a subject. This makes them especially useful for close-up shots, such as photos of insects, jewelry, or coins. They are also used to copy documents or material from books.

Zoom lenses, the most popular type of special lenses, are actually many lenses in one. They are variable focal length lenses. With a zoom lens, a photographer can stand in one position and vary the magnification of the subject without stopping to change the lens. Some typical ranges for zoom lenses are 80-200mm; 75-260mm; 50-300mm; and 200-600mm. Some zoom lenses are also macro lenses, making them some of the most useful lenses yet designed for the average photographer.

fisheye lenses cause extreme distortion

Supplementary Lenses

A supplementary lens is one that is attached either in front of or behind the existing lens. One type of supplementary device, the tele-extender, can increase the effective focal length of the lens attached to it by two or three times. The tele-extender is placed on the camera body, and then the lens is attached to it. A 2X extender (converter) will double the focal length of the lens. For instance, a normal 50mm lens attached to a 2X converter will make it a 100mm telephoto. A 3X converter will triple the power. A 50mm attached to a 3X converter will make it a 150mm lens. The tele-extender is useful because it gives the photographer a telephoto lens inexpensively. However, it absorbs considerable light. A 2X converter will require opening the lens two more stops. A 3X converter requires three more f-stop openings. A tele-converter also will reduce the sharpness of the lens being used with it.

Fig. 10-6

use lens tissue for thorough cleaning

Another type of supplementary lens is the Plus lens or close-up lens. These are actually more like filters, because they screw onto the front of the regular lens. Plus lenses come in various powers. The Plus 1, Plus 2, and Plus 3 lenses allow the photographer to get increasingly closer to a subject without being out of focus. They can also be used in combination. For instance, you can make a Plus 6 lens by using a Plus 1, Plus 2, and Plus 3 all together. One thing to keep in mind when using close-up lenses is depth of field. The closer you are to the subject, the less depth of field. Plus lenses are not as sharp as a macro lens used at the same distance. However, because of their cost, they are more popular.

Care of Lenses

Most good lenses are made of glass and are susceptible to scratching. A scratch on a lens may reduce its sharpness. Protective lens caps are made for both the front and back of a lens. If the lens is not in use, it should be protected with a rear lens cap as well as one on the front.

use a camel's hair brush to dust lens

Lenses must also be free from dirt, dust, or fingerprints, since these will all cut down the sharpness. Cleaning a lens requires care because the glass is so easily scratched. A camel's hair brush is used to clean any dust or lint from the surface of the lens, while tissue is used to wipe away dirt. Use the lens tissue with a circular motion; (See Fig. 10-6) scrubbing with the tissue may scratch the lens. Be sure to use only tissue designed for camera lenses. Tissues for cleaning eyeglasses contain a cleaner that is harmful to the lens coating.

For fingerprints use a commercial lens cleaner. These are solvents that dissolve away the fingerprints without too much rubbing with the lens tissue.

Many photographers like to keep either a UV (ultraviolet) or 1a (skylight) filter on the camera lens at all times to protect the lens from scratches and dust.

Assignment: Lenses

1. What is the purpose of the camera lens? Why does a camera need a lens at all, since you can make a photograph with a pin-hole camera which has no lens?
2. Review the effects of depth of field. Focal length of the camera is one of the factors that affects depth of field. How does a long focal length lens affect the overall appearance of a photograph? What effect does a long focal length lens have on depth of field? How does a shorter than normal focal length lens affect the over-all photograph? How does a shorter than normal focal length lens affect depth of field?
3. Through the use of accuracy lenses such as wide-angle, tele-photo, and close-up lenses, make a series of *at least* six photo-graphs that shows how expressive qualities (moods) can be changed from the way they are normally seen by the human eye or through a "normal" camera lens.

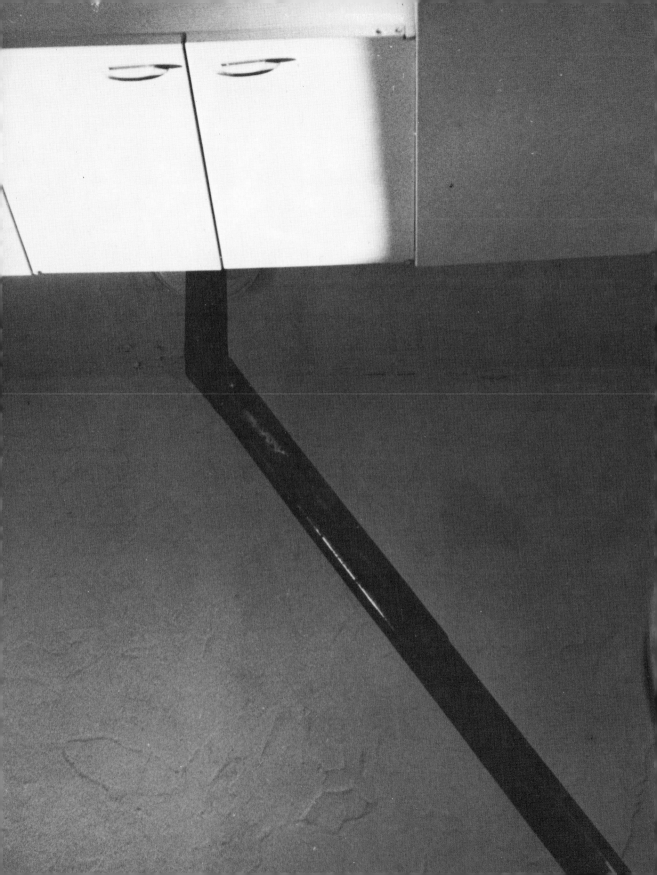

The Camera

11

The camera is the tool that enables a photographer to record a personal interpretation and viewpoint of reality. By artistic use of the camera, the photographer has a way of seeing, understanding and appreciating the visual world. By using the camera intelligently, the photographer can communicate these impressions to others.

As you learned from investigating the pinhole camera (Chapter 2), all cameras are basically similar. Each is a light-tight box with film at one end and a hole or lens to admit light at the opposite end. All cameras, regardless of cost, work in that manner. The differences are how well, how easily, and how flexibly they transmit light to the film to make an image.

There are hundreds of cameras available today. Choosing a camera can, and often does, become confusing. However, most cameras can be classified by their viewfinder systems. Rangefinder cameras provide a separate viewfinder for framing and focusing the shot. Most rangefinder cameras are held up to the eye and can be focused quickly. The rangefinder itself (see Chapter 3) consists of a pair of mirrors placed a few inches apart so that the eye sees a double or ghost image of the subject. The other mirror moves while the lens is being focused, so that when the subject is in focus, the two images are superimposed. Rangefinder cameras are made in several film sizes, the most popular being 35mm. Rangefinder cameras provide the brightest possible view of the subject, making them ideal for low-light situations. Also, they are quieter than a single-lens reflex.

Rangefinder cameras do, however, have certain disadvantages. Parallax (see Chapter 3) can occur because you are framing the photo through a separate viewing system, not through the lens. This problem is especially critical when working less than 2 feet from the subject. Another problem is the lack of versatility of most rangefinder cameras. Except in very expensive models, most rangefinder types cannot use interchangeable lenses. Even if the camera has lens interchangeability, a separate viewfinder must be

rangefinder

35mm

2¼ single-lens reflex

installed to see what the lens will see. Finally, many rangefinder cameras have built-in automatic exposure systems. This is a plus feature if working fast is important. However, the disadvantages of automatic exposure far outweigh their advantages. Unless the camera has a way of overriding the automation, it is best not to consider it for learning purposes.

The single-lens reflex (SLR) cameras provide the best way to seeing exactly what the camera lens sees. (See Chapter 4.) A system of prisms and mirrors lets you look right through the lens. Viewing your subject through the lens, you can see the depth of field and frame precisely what will be included in the photograph and what will not. Single-lens reflex cameras are made in different film formats, the most popular using 35mm or roll film such as 120 film.

The single-lens reflex camera has several advantages over the rangefinder. For instance, parallax is no longer a problem since the camera allows for viewing through the lens. Also, many SLR's offer interchangeable lenses. However, they too have their disadvantages, the main one being weight.

The SLR in most cases weighs more than the rangefinder and is usually less compact, although manufacturers are working to solve this problem. They are also more complex mechanically than the rangefinder, and so the potential for broken or out-of-order parts is greater. Because the mirror in an SLR must move out of the way to make the exposure on the film, they are also noisier than other types of cameras. This can be a problem in photographing animals or self-conscious people. Finally, because the light bounces off several points inside the camera before it reaches your eye, and because each one of these points absorbs some light, it is often hard to focus in dim light and with slow lenses. This is one reason why rangefinders are popular with many photographers. Even with these disadvantages, the SLR has become the most popular focusing system in better quality cameras.

Many photographers prefer to compose their images on a large flat ground glass, rather than at eye level. A twin-lens reflex (TLR) allows the photographer to turn a three-dimensional scene into a two-dimensional image, which is the way all scenes are rendered in a photograph. Like the rangefinder camera, the twin-lens reflex has a viewing system separate from the lens. However, like the single-lens reflex (from which it developed), the TLR uses a mirror that reflects the image of the scene onto a viewing screen or ground glass (see Chapter 3). Most twin-lens reflex cameras use roll film, either 120 or 220. (220 film does not have a paper backing like 120. Because of that, more film is contained on the same size spool, so that more exposures can be made. Not all 120 cameras can use 220 film, however, mainly because there must be an automatic exposure counter to show how many pictures have been taken, without numbers on the paper backing.)

The TLR camera, because the mirror is stationary, is quieter than the SLR. Its ground glass is much larger than in eye-level cameras, making it easier to focus and to compose the picture. Since the photographer looks down into the camera, it can be set on the ground for compositional effects or to photograph low subjects, such as pets or babies. Another advantage of the TLR is the film size used. A 2¼″ x 2¼″ is four times the area of a 35mm negative. Thus, a bigger enlargement can be made from it. Unless you can buy an expensive SLR that uses large roll film producing a negative 2¼″ x 2¼″ or larger, the TLR is probably your best choice.

2¼ twin-lens reflex

The major problems with the twin-lens reflex are parallax, size, speed, viewing, and versatility. Parallax is a problem except in the best of these cameras. Because most TLR's use a large film size, they are bigger and more cumbersome to carry around. Another problems is that while they provide a large, flat viewing screen for focusing and composing, the image on the screen is reversed, left to right. It takes practice to compensate for this. Another drawback is that most of these cameras do not offer lens interchangeability. However, for those people who like to photograph scenery, architecture, or still-lifes, or who simply want a larger negative for better enlarging quality, the TLR should be considered.

The view camera has the advantages of both a through-the-lens viewing system and a large negative size. If the photographer works precisely and methodically and wants a sharp, high quality negative, the view camera is considered ideal. View cameras work like an accordion, with a lens in front and a ground glass viewing screen opposite the lens. They are focused by moving the lens back and forward. The view camera is the ideal choice for product illustrations, super-sharp close-ups, portraits, and studio photography. It is also the choice for the photographer who wants to control distortion, because the film plane and lens can be tilted, raised, and lowered. No camera is better for architectural work.

All view cameras use film that is cut to a particular size, called cut film or sheet film. The most popular size is 4″ x 5″, although it comes as large as 11″ x 14″. Such a large negative produces an excellent print, assuming all the other variables are constant.

The view camera, however, is not the ideal choice for all types of photography, especially when speed is important. A tripod must be used because of the camera's size and weight. The image on the viewing screen is not bright. Photographers often drape a dark cloth over the camera to block out strong light so they can see to focus better. Also, the image on the viewfinder is reversed and upside down. Getting used to that is also a problem. Finally, there is the cut film itself, which must be loaded by the photographer into sheet film holders. Each holder, however, can hold only one piece of film on each side, giving only two exposures for each holder. The photographer who uses a view camera generally must carry a number of holders to take several exposures. Because of these

modern Polaroid

Pocket-Instamatic®

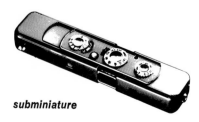

subminiature

problems, the view camera is seldom used except for studio work. Nevertheless, if you want the highest quality negative and are willing to sacrifice speed and convenience, the view camera, when used properly, has no equal. Remember, though, that view cameras are not really useful for candid portraits, for shooting with available light, or in any other situation that requires speed.

Other Camera Types

Certain kinds of cameras cannot be classified by type of viewfinder. These usually use special kinds of film. These cameras are (1) sub-miniature, (2) Instamatic-type, and (3) Polaroid. The tiny sub-miniature camera was developed as a high-precision instrument for espionage work during World War II. After the war, they became popular with the general public. Some of them are as small as a pack of gum. Because of their size, they produce a very small negative, some of them four times smaller than a 35mm negative. Sub-miniatures are useful because you can carry them in a pocket or purse. However, they require special equipment for processing and, at best, do not yield a very good quality print much larger than 3½" x 5".

When the concept of Instamatic® photography was introduced in 1963 by the Eastman Kodak Company, it virtually eliminated film-loading problems for even the most amateur photographer. After the original 126 film-size Instamatic was introduced, another smaller film size, the 110 or Pocket Instamatic®, was developed. Both Instamatic-type cameras use cartridge-loaded film that is dropped into the camera. The least expensive of these cameras are basically "box cameras." That is, their lenses are quite crude, they are pre-focused at about 8 feet, and they have only two shutter speeds, one for flash and the other for outdoor use. The more expensive cartridge-load cameras have better optics as well as devices for focusing. Some also have automatic exposure systems, which, when combined with a good lens and focusing, will yield a fairly good negative. However, even the best Instamatic®-type camera will not yield as good a negative and print as a good 35mm properly used.

When George Eastman named his first camera the "Kodak," the name caught on until it became a household word synonymous with photography. And when Dr. Edwin H. Land introduced his Polaroid Land® camera in the late 1940s, that name became synonymous around the world with instant-picture photography. There are many different Polaroid® models, varying in cost and features. They use only Polaroid® film, which is available in both black and white and color. Some of these films yield a fully processed black-and-white negative and positive in a matter of minutes. Some of the more sophisticated Polaroid® cameras, which do not have built-in automatic exposure systems, are used by professional photographers to check composition, lighting, and the like. Some excellent photographers, like Ansel Adams, have produced very high quality prints with Polaroid equipment. A recently published book, *Singular Images* by Adams, illustrates what can be accomplished using Polaroid film.

Used Equipment

Many photographers cannot afford a new camera, and so they turn to used equipment. By shopping carefully, they can probably find a fairly recent model in good condition at a reasonable price. Although some photographers think they must have all the latest features, this is not really true. Although you may, when buying a used camera, end up with someone else's troubles, most photo dealers are reliable and will let you return a used camera if it is not working right. Usually a camera is sold either because its owner didn't understand how to use it, or because it was old and didn't have all the latest features.

When buying a used camera, look it over for signs of misuse. Dents in the body or around the lens rim indicate that the camera has been dropped. In that case, ask the dealer if the camera is sold with a warranty. Look at the lens to see if it is free from scratches caused by overzealous cleaning. After you have purchased or rented a used camera, shoot a roll of film immediately. After development, check the negatives to see if there are any scratches on them. These indicate a dirty pressure plate. Make sure the focusing is accurate and the lens is of good quality by enlarging part of the negative. If the camera passes all these tests, and the price is reasonable, it probably is a good buy.

Instamatic®

Camera Care

The camera you are using is a fine, precision instrument. It was made with great care and contains a great many moving parts, which must work in harmony. Continual attention to your camera is primarily common sense care. The following are some basic tips for keeping your camera in good condition.

STORAGE—When the camera is not in use, it should be protected from dust, preferably in a case. Avoid storing the camera in excessively hot, cold, or damp places. Normal room temperature is best. Always attach a body cap when the camera body is to be stored separately. Never leave the shutter or self-timer cocked if the camera is to be stored overnight or longer. Remove any batteries if the camera is not to be used for several weeks. Batteries can leak causing corrosion.

CAMERA BODY—Brush the inside of the camera periodically using a soft brush. This is especially important after you have used the camera on a beach, or other conditions where dust or sand can infiltrate into the mechanism. If you have an SLR, keep the mirror free from fingerprints and dust.

USAGE—Keep the camera away from water. Avoid excessive moisture. If the camera is to be used near water, guard it against splashes, especially from salt water. If some lever or turning part does not move with the usual pressure, do not force it. If this happens, it is usually caused by an oversight in the sequence of operation. The shutter will not trip, for example, unless it is cocked, or unless the film is advanced in an automatic cocking camera. No amount of pressure on the shutter release will activate the shutter. When all steps of operations have been checked, and the mechanism still does not operate with normal pressure, it's time to see a camera repairman.

Camera Manufacturers and Distributors

All camera manufacturers or their distributors supply information about their particular line of equipment. Simply write them a letter asking for information. You may also want to stop in your local camera shop, where you can get information of a different sort. There, most camera salespeople will be happy to discuss camera models with you.

ARGUS
Argus, Inc.
2080 Lunt Ave.
Elk Grove Village, Ill. 60007

BRONICA
Ehrenrich Photo-Optical Co
623 Stewart Ave.
Garden City, N.Y. 11530

CANON
Canon U.S.A.
10 Nevada Dr.
Lake Success, N.Y. 11040

EASTMAN KODAK
Eastman Kodak
343 State St.
Rochester, N.Y. 14650

FUJICA
Fuji Film U.S.A.
350 5th Ave.
New York, N.Y. 10001

GAF
GAF
140 51st St.
New York, N.Y. 10020

HANIMEX PRACTICKA
Hanimex (U.S.A.) Inc.
7020 Lawndale Ave.
Chicago, Ill. 60645

HASSELBLAD
Pillard Inc.
1900 Lower Rd.
Linden, N.J. 07036

HONEYWELL PENTAX
Honeywell Photographic
Dept. 102-465
P.O. Box 22083
Denver, Colo. 80222

KOWA
Same address as Konica

KONICA
Berkey Photo
25-20 Brooklyn-Queens Expwy.
   West
Woodside, N.Y. 11377

LEICA
E. Leitz, Inc.
Rockleigh Industrial Park
Rockleigh, N.J. 07647

MIRANDA
Interstate Photo Supply
168 Glen Cove Road
Carle Place, N.Y. 11514

MINOLTA
Minolta Corp.
101 Williams Drive
Ramsey, N.J. 07466

MAMIYA/SEKOR
Bell & Howell
7235 Linder Ave.
Skokie, Illinois 60076

Assignment: The Camera

1. What are the basic parts of any camera, including the pinhole camera?
2. The two most popular camera types used by photographers are the rangefinder and the single-lens reflex. Contrast these two camera types in terms of the following:
   a. focusing methods,
   b. path of light from subject to the photographer's eye,
   c. brightness of image in the viewfinder,
   d. type of shutter,
   e. weight and bulk,
   f. availability and use of accessory lenses.

NIKON/NIKKORMAT
Same address as Bronica

LINHOF
Same address as Konica

OLYMPUS
Ponder & Best
1630 Stewart St.
Santa Monica, Calif. 90406

PETRI
Petri International
150 Great Neck Rd.
Great Neck, N.Y. 11021

POLAROID
Polaroid Corp.
549 Technology Sq.
Cambridge, Mass. 02139

RICOH
Ricoh of America
6 Kingsbridge Rd.
Fairfield, N.J. 67006

ROLLEI
Rollei U.S.A.
100 Lehigh Dr.
Fairfield, N.J. 07006

TOPCON
Same adress as Hasselblad

VIVITAR
Same address as Olympus

YASHICA
Yashica Inc.
50-17 Queens Blvd.
Woodside, N.Y. 11377

Introduction to Color Photography

12

Imagine that there were no color in the world. Every object, every place or person that we see would suddenly become a shade of gray. How would that change affect us? Color is one dimension by which we measure time and identify objects and places. The color of light on a scene alters as the day moves from sunrise to sunset and as the seasons pass from spring to autumn, from winter to summer. We identify most objects with their colors—apples are red, leaves are green, the sky is blue. Without color we would have to rely on the shape of the object, its smell, taste, size, weight, and other characteristics.

In photography, the dimension of color adds to the visual impact of the photograph on the viewer. When used knowledgeably, color adds to the esthetic appeal and meaning of a photograph.

Color photography is a complex process that we accept casually without realizing what a recent development it is. Research into the theory of color began as early as 1666, when Sir Isaac Newton first demonstrated that light is the source for all color. But the first colored photographs were simply black-and-white photographs hand-painted with colors. Even Daguerreotypes, whose tonal range has never been equalled, were not spared from mutilation by untrained painters. The world longed for a mechanical color process that would represent the colors of life, avoiding the interpretations of untrained painters.

Not until the early 20th century did true color processes become available. The most popular of these early techniques was Autochrome, invented in France by Auguste and Louis Lumiere. They introduced the process commercially in 1908, although the American photographic pioneers Alfred Stieglitz and Edward Steichen both photographed with Autochrome in 1907. An Autochrome is one glass plate with a positive colored image. Because it is a positive and on glass, one must hold it to light for it to be visible. It is called a transparency since light must be transmitted through the glass for the image to be seen. A viewing device, known as a diascope held the Autochrome at an angle so that light could be transmitted through the glass plate. The image was reflected to

Diascope

the viewer by a mirror inside the diascope. Autochromes had many disadvantages—long exposure time, the need for the diascope, and most important, the difficulties of handling the process itself.

Almost 30 years passed before an easy-to-use color film was produced. Invented by two musician-scientists, Leopold Mannes and Leopold Godowsky, Jr., the first Kodachrome film was introduced on April 15, 1935. It had three emulsion layers, each sensitive to a different color. Kodachrome dye formers are incorporated in the developers and dyes are formed and added to the film during processing. The first Kodachrome film was made for amateur movie-making; later it was made in 35mm and sheet film.

How Color Is Created

In photography, there are two basic ways of creating color that will match the color of all visible objects. One method is *additive*, the other *subtractive*. The basic underlying principle of both methods is that the color of any object can be matched by appropriate mixtures of red, green, and blue light. Remember that we are using light, not paint. Red, green, and blue are the *primary colors* of light because the right combination of them can match any known color. (The primary paint, or pigment, colors are magenta, yellow, and cyan.) When each of the primary light colors is present in equal intensity, we see white light. In the absence of light—when no colors are present—we see black.

The additive color process starts with the three primary colors of light and adds together different amounts of each one to produce some other color. The subtractive color process is demonstrated by transmitting white light through a color filter. The filter's complementary color will be subtracted. For example, a green filter subtracts red from white light.

The first public demonstration showing how colored light could be added together to make a color photograph was given in 1861 by British physicist James Clerk Maxwell. His experiment is quite valuable in understanding this color process. Because the experiment is somewhat complex, it is suggested that you try it with several other students. To do the experiment you will need a camera (preferably 35mm) loaded with black and white panchromatic film, three slide projectors, three filters—medium red, medium blue, and medium green—and finally, a good test subject. The best subject is a color wall chart from an art supply shop or paint store. Fasten the color chart to a flat surface and then aim the camera at the chart.

For the first exposure, use a red filter over the lens; for the second, a green filter; and for the third, a blue filter. Calculate the exposure for each according to the filter factors. After the exposures are made, develop the film. As you look at each negative, you will see that the film records the chart in terms of the light transmitted by the filter. Where the color block is not solid red, green, or blue, but a mixture, each negative may have recorded it. In other words, the three negatives are silver records on film of the amounts of each primary color in the color chart.

These negatives are called *separation negatives* because they separate each of the three primary colors onto a separate negative. Now print the negatives onto three other pieces of the same type of black-and-white film. (For convenience, use contact printing.) Develop these positives and examine them. You'll notice that the clear spaces in each positive image represent the corresponding primary color in the chart. The dense portions of the negative show the areas where that primary color is missing.

Next mount each of the three positives into a separate holder that will fit into a slide projector. Insert each one in a separate slide projector, placing the corresponding colored filter over the projector lens. Aim all the projectors at a white screen from the same distance.

Individually, each projects only one color. Projector A shows only those parts of the chart that are red, projector B, those parts that are green, and projector C, the blue. Now move the projectors so that they produce one image in perfect register on the screen. This one image is a full-color likeness of the color chart. The red and green projected together make yellow; blue and green make cyan; and blue and red make magenta. Yet when all are projected together, in register, they form a full-color reproduction of the original. By adding the primary colors together, you were able to reproduce an infinite variety of colors with the additive color process.

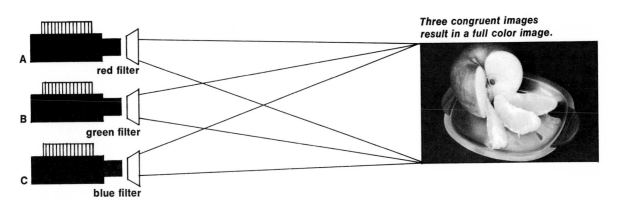

Three congruent images result in a full color image.

A   red filter

B   green filter

C   blue filter

Subtractive Color Process

Not long after Clerk Maxwell demonstrated the additive color process, two Frenchmen working independently discovered, almost simultaneously, another process. In 1869 Charles Cros and Louis Ducos du Hauron each announced the subtractive color process, the method that became the basis of present-day color photography. It involves creating colors by combining dyed images instead of mixing colored lights as in the additive process.

cyan filter blocks out red light

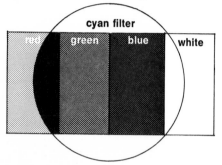

magenta filter blocks out green light

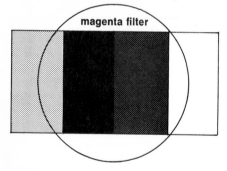

yellow filter blocks out blue light

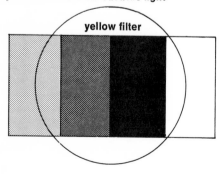

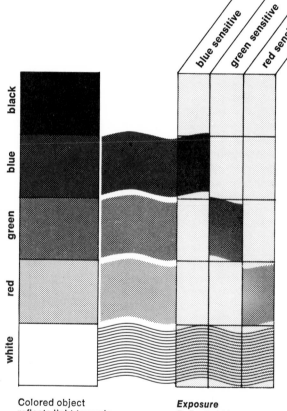

Colored object
reflects light towards
camera

Exposure
Reflected blue,
green, and red light
is recorded on
emulsions sensitive
to blue, green, and
red light.
White light is
recorded on all three
emulsions.
Black (no light) is
not recorded.

Like the additive method, the subtractive process uses three black-and-white negatives, each one representing the red, green, or blue in a subject. But, the positives made from these negatives are not black and white. Instead, they are transformed by a series of complex steps into an image made of dye. These images are then superimposed to create a full-color photograph. In other words, colors have been subtracted from white light, leaving an image of the desired color. The subtractive process has become the most successful method of obtaining full-color photographs.

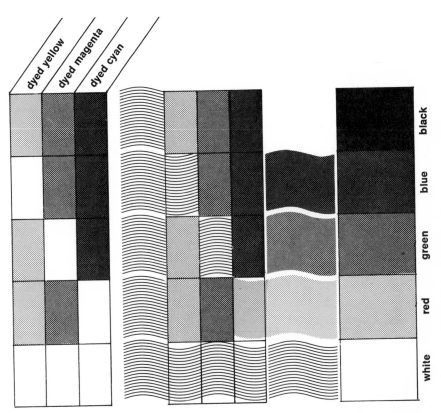

First Development
A negative silver image of each color is formed in parts of each layer.

Second Development
The film is exposed a second time, sensitizing the silver remaining in other parts of the emulsions. Each emulsion is dyed a color complementary to the color it recorded. The negative silver image formed in the first development is washed away.

Projection
As white light passes through transparent combinations of primary colors (primary pigment colors), the original colors are remixed.

Projected Image
Magenta and cyan dyes transmit blue. Yellow and cyan dyes transmit green. Yellow and magenta dyes transmit red. Yellow, magenta, and cyan dyes block out all colors, resulting in black.

Processing Color Film

Modern color photography uses the subtractive process, but color film is of two types. Color reversal film produces slides, or transparencies. Color negative film produces prints. All color film has three emulsion layers. Each layer is basically similar to black-and-white film except that it is sensitive to one primary color (red, green, or blue).

Color Reversal Processes

Reversal color processes produce color transparencies, which can be viewed only when light passes through them. A slide projector enlarges the small color transparency into a size that may even be larger than the original subject.

The two most popular color reversal films are Kodachrome and Ektachrome, both made by Eastman Kodak. However, there are other brands available. The Kodachrome process is probably the most often used. The film itself was originally a three-layer sandwich, with each layer sensitive to a primary color. During processing, chemicals reverse the negative image to a positive. It is then redeveloped, adding one of the cyan, magenta, and yellow dyes to each layer of emulsion. Because the color is added during processing, Kodachrome cannot be handled in most darkrooms. In fact, many countries do not have a single darkroom equipped for this process.

Kodachrome® is manufactured for popular film sizes, 35mm, 126, 110, and 828. There are presently two types of daylight Kodachrome® available, KM and KR. KM has an ASA of 25 while KR has an ASA of 64.

Ektachrome®, like Kodachrome® has three emulsion layers sandwiched together. However, in Ektachrome® the color dyes are incorporated in the film layers and do not have to be added during processing. Because of this, Ektachrome can be developed in any darkroom. Ektachrome® also is presently made in two speeds—Ektachrome-X® with an ASA of 64 and high-speed Ektachrome (EH)® with an ASA of 160. EH® is ideal for shooting color in available light.

Negative-Positive Color Process

The negative-positive relationship in color is essentially the same as in black-and-white photography. A negative is first exposed and developed, after which it is either contact printed or enlarged on photographic paper. Color negative film works much like color reversal film except that it produces a negative image—light areas appear dark; dark areas, light; and the colors appear as their complementary hues. The paper for printing color negatives consists of three layers, each sensitive to a primary color, thus it will produce a positive color print.

Although several companies make color negative film, the most popular are those made by Eastman Kodak. Of the Kodak films, the most popular is Kodacolor II® (CII), which has an ASA of 80 and is available in most film sizes. Ektacolor® (CPS) and Vericolor II® (VPS) have a slightly higher ASA of 100. Both Ektacolor® and Vericolor® can be processed and printed in most well-equipped darkrooms. Color negative film can also be printed as black-and-white positives by using a panchromatic paper like Panalure,® which translates color in terms of the black-and-white tonal scale.

Color and Light

In color photography, the color of the light source becomes an important consideration. Different light sources have different dominant colors. Daylight, for example, is dominantly blue, while artificial indoor light (incandescent) is more red. The eye is not aware of these distinctions because the brain remembers the way a color "ought to" look and compensates for changes. However, color film "sees" color as it really is. Therefore different types of color film are made for different picture-taking situations.

A light source's relative warmness (reds and yellows) or coolness (greens and blues) is designated by its *color temperature,* measured in degrees Kelvin. In this system, light is measured in terms of its warmness and coolness. The cooler the color, the higher the Kelvin number (or K). For example, Kodachrome® Type A film is balanced for 3400K; whereas Ektachrome® Type B is balanced for 3200K. Therefore, type A film is corrected for a cooler light source than type B.

Because films vary in color sensitivity, color filters are needed if a film is to be used with a light source other than the one for which it was balanced. These are called conversion filters or color corrections.

Successful color prints or slides require careful consideration of both exposure and light conditions. The wrong light source can give the photograph an objectionable color cast. The wrong exposure can yield a color that is too pale or too dark.

The photographer must also be aware that a color photograph must be composed as carefully as a black-and-white shot. Color alone will not carry the message or make a good photograph.

Richard Bresden

Assignment: Introduction to Color Photography

1. Try the experiment described in this chapter. As the text suggests, the experiment is complex and should probably be done by a group of students as a class demonstration, or as a project for an entire class. This experiment will help you understand the color process.

2. What is "color temperature"? What changes must be made when you are taking color photographs under incandescent light, fluorescent light, and daylight? Are the emulsions of all color films equally sensitive to the same colors?

3. You can begin to increase your awareness of small changes in color if you will try the following experiment. Have two or more members of the class shoot a 20-exposure roll of color slide film made by different manufacturers. Shoot all the pictures under the same type of light even though the film may not be specifically designed for that type of light. Keep a record of the lighting conditions for each photograph (your slides will be returned to you numbered in sequence). Set up one slide projector for each group of slides and project them at the same time. The entire class should participate in an evaluation of the effects of different kinds of light upon the quality of the color in the photographs. Compare the difference in color you may see between different kinds of film, even though all the pictures were shot with the same type of light.

The History of Photography 13

Photography is not a natural phenomenon; it has its basis in science and thus it had to be invented. And because of the value of photography today, it seems surprising that it took so long to be developed. The invention wasn't simply a matter of someone making a camera and putting some film into it for the first time. It evolved over hundreds of years and was much like a jigsaw puzzle. One man would make a small discovery and another man, years later, would build upon that discovery, until the pieces of information finally fit together.

The Camera

There is no way of knowing who constructed the first camera or, as it is called in Latin, the *camera obscura*. (The principle was known to the Arabian scholar Ibn Al Haitham before 1038.) In its basic form, the camera obscura was a dark chamber or room. Light passed through a small hole at one end of the room and formed an image on the opposite wall. This image was not sharp, as no lenses were attached to the opening in the wall. However, the smaller the hole, the sharper the image, as in pinhole photography. In 1558 Giovanni Pattista della Porta described the camera obscura at length. He was also the first to suggest that the camera obscura be used as a guide for drawing, and it is for this that he is remembered. The application of lenses to camera obscuras (by 1550) increased both the sharpness and brightness of the image and led to further investigations into the design and construction of camera obscuras.

As more people became interested in them, the size of camera obscuras shrunk until they became extremely portable (by comparison) and could be used by more people as a help in rendering perspective correctly. In 1676 the first "reflex" camera appeared—for example, one in which the image is reflected onto a top-mounted viewing screen by an inclined mirror behind the lens. All the artist had to do was put a piece of tracing paper on top of the viewing screen and trace his outline. Thus the camera became part of the artist's tools.

Camera obscura used by artists to expedite their drawings.

Hunter and His Dog. Half plate Ambrotype by unknown American photographer, c. 1858. (Mark Jacobs Collection)

151

Photographic Chemistry

Photographic chemistry came rather late in the long history of the development of the camera. Photographic chemistry refers to the invention of a light sensitive material, an emulsion. The first important discovery was made by Johann Heinrich Schulze, a professor of anatomy at the University of Altorf near Nuremberg.

In 1725 Schulze saturated chalk with nitric acid that contained some silver. Exposing this mixture to the sun, Schulze was amazed to discover that the mixture facing the sun turned dark violet while the portion turned away from the sun remained white. At first he believed that the darkening was due to the mixture of chalk and nitric acid, but he failed to repeat this experiment. Some time later he remembered that the mixture had contained silver, as well as chalk and nitric acid. Finally realizing that it was the silver and nitric acid that caused the darkening by light, Schulze prepared more concentrated solutions until he was able to form words on the bottles containing the solutions by stenciling out letters and exposing the bottles to direct sunlight. Although Schulze mentioned that it was possible to spread the silver solution on skin, bone, and wood to produce images, he did not do it. At this time there was no way to make these stencils permanent, and they soon faded away.

Permanent Image

The next important discovery was made by the Swedish chemist Carl Wilhelm Scheele. Scheele confirmed one of Schulze's discoveries: that the blackening effect of the silver salts was due to light and not to heat. To prove this he spread the white compound on paper and exposed it to the sun for two weeks, during which the paper turned completely black. He then poured ammonia on the powder and discovered that the blackened silver was metallic silver and had become insoluble in ammonia; that is, the ammonia did not dissolve the exposed silver. The ammonia, in other words, acted as a fixer. Scheele did not realize the importance of his discovery—the ability to make a photographic image permanent. Nor did Scheele conceive the idea of photography, an honor reserved for the Englishman Thomas Wedgewood.

Thomas Wedgewood, the youngest son of Josiah, the famous potter, was brought up in a scientific atmosphere. The exact dates of his experiments in photography are not known, although they are presumed to be around 1800. Wedgewood did not succeed in making the images he exposed through a camera obscura permanent; so none of them survive today. Although Wedgewood was familiar with Scheele's work, neither Wedgewood nor Scheele realized the importance of the ammonia fixer. Wedgewood was the first, however, to conceive the idea of photography with the use of a portable camera obscura.

The world's first permanent camera image done from nature was made by a Frenchman, Joseph Nicephore Niepce, at his family's estate near Chalon in 1826. The culmination of an experiment begun ten years earlier, it began the long history of contributions to the development of photography by artists, as Niepce was by trade a lithographer, which in 1813 was a new art. (Lithography is a process whereby a drawing, made with a grease pencil on limestone, can be printed on paper many times over. It began as a method of reproduction and soon became an art form in its own right. After the drawing is made on the limestone, the stone must be treated with a series of chemicals before it is ready to be printed.)

Niepce's son, Isidore, made the drawings on the stone while his father attended to the chemical process. They soon switched to using pewter instead of stone (the material on which the first photograph was made) because limestone was difficult to get locally. The next year Isidore joined the army, which caused a problem since Joseph Niepce was not able to draw very well. It was at this point that Niepce began to look for a way to make the action of light etch the pictures into the pewter plate.

Heliography

It is important to note that Niepce did not set out to make a photograph; he set out to make a photo-lithograph, trying to reproduce copies of drawings and paintings, which he succeeded in doing in 1822. He called his process heliography (sunwriting). In 1826 Niepce succeeded in making the first permanent photograph from nature using a camera obscura. The "heliograph" was made on a pewter plate, and it took eight hours for the image to be recorded!

In that same year Niepce received a letter from a Parisian painter, Louis Jacques Mande Daguerre, who worked primarily with oils. Daguerre mentioned that he, too, had been working with light images and asked Niepce about his progress. Niepce was at first very cautious in replying to Daguerre, but after Daguerre visited him and the two men corresponded further, they formed a partnership in 1829. Their partnership, however, did not produce any noticeable improvement in making photography practicable. In 1833 Niepce—the inventor of photography—died.

Daguerre made photography practical. He improved the process so much that he felt justified in naming the product the "Daguerreotype." In August 1839 the French government honored Daguerre with a life pension and gave to the world, as public property, the Daguerreotype process—everywhere, that is, except England, where Daguerre had secretly patented the process.

The Daguerreotype

The process of Daguerre was as follows. A sheet of copper was plated with silver—the silver surface being well cleaned and highly polished. The silver surface was exposed, in a small box, to iodine vapor until the surface was a golden yellow. The sensitized surface was then placed in a camera obscura, where it remained for five or six minutes. It was then taken from the camera and developed in a vapor derived from mercury. Then the plate was washed and dried, after which it was placed in a case with a sheet of glass over the Daguerreotype to protect its surface, as it is very easy to rub the image off the plate.

A well-exposed Daguerreotype is possibly the most beautiful form of photography. It possesses brilliance because of the silver surface and shows detail far better than any modern paper print. Of course, there are some outstanding defects in a Daguerreotype. The image can be seen only when it is held in a certain position; otherwise it simply reflects light over its surface because of its mirrorlike quality. Another defect of the Daguerreotype was that only one copy of the image could be made from each exposure.

Even with these defects, the Daguerreotype was the most important photographic process for more than fifteen years, and especially in America, where many improvements were made. The most important improvement was the shorter exposure time it took to make the image. At first the exposure time needed to make a Daguerreotype was five to twenty minutes—too long to make portraits feasible. But by the end of 1840 several Americans had made significant improvements, so that the exposure time was cut to a few seconds. This, of course, made portraits possible, and by 1841 the first "chain" of portrait galleries was opened—by John Plumbe. There were also men who taught the art of the Daguerreotype, the most notable of whom was Samuel F. B. Morse, the inventor of the telegraph, who had met Daguerre in Paris while demonstrating his invention.

The list of those who studied under Morse reads like a Who's Who of photography: Edward Anthony, who started the photographic supply house E. Anthony and Company (which later became Ansco and now is known as GAF); Albert S. Southworth, who started the firm of Southworth and Hawes and was the best of the Daguerrian artists; and Mathew Brady, who opened his own chain of Daguerrian galleries (and, of course, documented the Civil War). Because of his teaching record, Samuel Morse earned the title Father of American Photography.

The Calotype

Men from all corners of the world praised Daguerre and his wonderful invention, never mentioning Niepce as the true inventor. Yet there was one man who heard the news with dismay. An English

Police Constable. ¼ plate daguerreotype by unknown American photographer, c. 1855. (Mark Jacobs Collection)

country gentleman, William Henry Fox Talbot, saw Daguerre's method as a threat to his own process, the calotype—or, as it was known later, the Talbotype. Talbot began his experiments in 1834 after returning from a trip to Italy, where he drew landscapes. His first successful images, made in 1835, were of leaves and lace laid down on sensitized paper and fixed in salt water, which was also Daguerre's first method. (These are negative images on paper, today referred to as "photograms.") Talbot made very little progress in the next three years because his attention was diverted to other matters. It was not until he received news of the impending announcement of Daguerre's method that he sought his place of honor. His actions from then on appear not to be those of an English gentleman.

Less than two weeks after the French government released the news of the Daguerreotype, Talbot visited John Frederick William Herschel, a prominent mathematician, astronomer, and chemist who was interested in photography from a chemist's viewpoint. Herschel was a generous man, and when Talbot visited him he described in detail a chemical he had invented which he called hyposulphite of soda. (This chemical is still in use today, known as "fixer." It makes photographic negatives and prints permanent.)

Talbot, on the other hand, revealed nothing of his process. He immediately put Herschel's "hypo" to use, and when Talbot wrote to the French government of his method, Daguerre immediately applied it to his own process.

Herschel not only discovered fixer, he coined the word photography, which comes from the Greek words meaning "light writing." Herschel used the term to differentiate between Talbot's negative paper prints and Daguerre's positive image method that used copper plates.

The calotype process could not compete with the Daguerreotype for several reasons. But perhaps the worst stumbling block in its evolution was Talbot himself, who patented the process and its improvements and sold them upon receipt of a large amount of money. However, Talbot must receive the credit for inventing the photographic process we use today—that is, the negative-positive relationship.

In 1847, eight years after Daguerre and Talbot made public their discoveries and fourteen years after Joseph Niepce died, a cousin of the latter, Abel Niepce de Saint-Victor, invented a process for sensitizing a glass plate with an emulsion of silver iodide and fresh, whipped eggwhite (albumin). The mixture was not very sensitive to light but it was capable of rendering fine detail and good tone, which the calotype negative was unable to do. Talbot patented a slight modification of this albumin-on-glass process in 1849, even though this method used a glass negative instead of— as with Talbot's calotype—a negative made of paper.

The Wet–Collodin Process

Another, and more important, invention was made by an English sculptor, Frederick Scott Archer. Archer learned the calotype process in 1847 and decided to improve it. In March of 1851 he gave the world the "wet collodin" negative; but the advantage of the wet collodin process was difficult to obtain. A glass plate had to be cleaned, after which iodized collodin was poured on the plate, which was then immersed in a silver-nitrate bath and put into the camera while still wet. Development had to be performed before the plate dried, and because of this it became known as the "wet plate" process. Again, Talbot claimed that the wet-plate process was an infringement upon his patented calotype, and he prosecuted anyone who didn't buy a license from him to use it. Finally, in December 1854, the courts found Talbot's claim illegal and released the process.

By 1858 the Daguerreotype was being replaced by the wet-collodin process. One variation of this process was known as the ambrotype, which was less difficult to make than the Daguerreotype. (An ambrotype is an underexposed wet-collodin negative on glass. When the ambrotype is mounted against a black backing,

Postmortem. ¼ plate-tintype by unknown American photographer, c. 1880. (Mark Jacobs Collection)

Family Portrait. ½ plate tintype by unknown American photographer, c. 1890. (Mark Jacobs Collection)

it appears like a positive.) Ambrotypes did not match the tonal range of a Daguerreotype, however, because they were quicker to make, they became very popular. But like the Daguerreotype, ambrotypes could not be duplicated; so copies could not be made.

The tintype was a variant of the ambrotype. Originally called a Ferrotype or Melainotype, they produced a positive image, usually on a thin sheet of iron (though some were made on leather and other materials). Tintypes were cheaper and easier to make than ambrotypes, and they were unbreakable. However, they lacked the tonal range of an ambrotype. Tintypes were made by the millions up to modern times.

Another type that was popular in the 1850s, along with the ambrotype, was the *cartes-de-visite,* a photographic visiting card. The fad began in France but soon was found almost everywhere: small photographs, about the size of a business card, with a portrait mounted to a cardboard backing. They were made by using a wet-plate negative, and thus any number of prints could be made. Because of this they were cheap and their popularity was enormous. (By 1860—with ambrotypes, tintypes, and *cartes-de-visite* being made at the same time—the Daguerreotype became a dead art.)

Mathew Brady

Mathew Brady, whose role in history began when he photographed the famous people of 1850 with the idea of publishing a book, *The Gallery of Illustrious Americans,* felt impelled to docu-

Mathew B. Brady: *Martin Van Buren. Half plate daguerreotype, c. 1856.*
(R. Bruce Duncan Collection)

ment the Civil War. Brady received President Lincoln's consent but no financial backing for that undertaking. However, Brady was a moderately wealthy man and had little reservation about spending his own money, thinking that after the war many people would buy prints of the battles. He assembled a staff of several men and outfitted them with the materials and equipment they needed to make wet-plate photographs. (Two of these men, Timothy O'Sullivan and Alexander Gardner, later became well known in their own right.) Brady himself very rarely left Washington, D.C., so that most of the picture taking was done by his assistants.

This enterprise left Mathew Brady practically destitute: people did not want to be reminded of the all-too-recent and horrible war. The negatives were stored in a warehouse and eventually auctioned off. In 1896 Brady died, penniless. Today, however, his negatives are priceless.

The South, too, had its photographers, such as George F. Cook of Charleston, South Carolina, who at one time was in charge of the Brady Gallery, and A. D. Lytle of Baton Rouge. (Lytle must have led the most dangerous life of all the photographers, for he would photograph Union forces and fortifications and forward his photos to Confederate headquarters.) For the most part, Southern photographers worked under greater hardships than Brady's men because their supplies had to be smuggled in from the North and Europe.

William H. Jackson

After the Civil War men began to be interested in the land west of the Mississippi. One cause for this was the photographs of the various Western regions taken by men such as Alexander Gardner (a Civil War photographer), John Carbutt of Chicago, T. H. O'Sullivan (one of Brady's crew), and William H. Jackson.

Jackson, perhaps the best known of these men, began to photograph the West with the Hayden survey in 1870, which chiefly followed the Oregon Trail through Wyoming. In 1871, Jackson was probably the first person to photograph the region that became known as Yellowstone National Park. The value of Jackson's photographs is verified by a bill that was introduced in Congress to set Yellowstone aside as a national park. His photos were put on exhibition the same time the bill was introduced, and for most of the men in Congress this was the first time they had ever "seen" the region. The bill was passed.

Several men photographed the American Indian around 1878, such as Adam Clark Vorman of San Francisco and L. A. Huffman of Montana. A little later another photographer of Indians, Edward S. Curtis, took some of the most beautiful portraits ever made.

One of the greatest portrait photographers of all time also worked with the wet-plate negative: Julia Margaret Cameron, who —although she had six children—began photography in 1863 at the

C. F. Watkins: *Galen Clark and the Grizzly Giant in Mariposa Grove, Big Trees, c. 1870.*
(R. Bruce Duncan Collection)

B 44 Section of the Grizzly Giant, 93 ft. diam., Mariposa Grove.
Watkins' New Boudoir Series, Yo Semite and Pacific Coast, 26 New Montgomery St., PALACE HOTEL, S F.

Confederate camp near Pensacola, Florida. Albumen print by unknown photographer, c. 1861.
(R. Bruce Duncan Collection)

W. H. Jackson. *Cabinet Card, c. 1880. (R. Bruce Duncan Collection)*

age of forty-eight. She taught herself photography, and although she was not technically well versed in it, her impressions of the great and famous men of England are far more important than her technical insufficiency. Her sitters included Lord Tennyson, Charles Darwin, and many children.

The Kodak

By 1880 the *wet* plate became dry, and thus a picture could be exposed and then developed weeks later. An amateur photographer of this period, George Eastman, became interested in the manufacture of dry plates. In December 1880 the Anthony Company (GAF today) began the sale of the Eastman dry plates. But some people began to dream of a flexible film. On September 4, 1888, Eastman patented a camera which was loaded with a roll of flexible film capable of 100 exposures. The camera sold for $25 and its slogan was "You press the button; we do the rest." It was named the Kodak.

When the 100 pictures were taken, the camera was mailed to the company, where (for $10) the film was removed and processed, prints were made, fresh film was reloaded, and the camera was returned to the sender with the finished prints.

The idea caught on, and in no time "Kodak" was a household name. Photography was now in the reach of everyone.

Photography as Art

The question "Is photography an art or a science?" is still very debatable. There is not a yes or no answer.

One figure who vigorously advanced the cause of photography as art was Alfred Stieglitz, who was born in Hoboken, New Jersey, in 1864. He spent his student years in Europe and was introduced to photography in 1883. He immediately became obsessed with photography, and constantly experimented with it while studying photo-chemistry at the Berlin Polytechnic. During the nine years he spent in Europe, he traveled, taking pictures wherever he went. By 1889 he was an internationally famous photographer.

Stieglitz returned to New York in 1890 and began publishing *Camera Notes,* a quarterly for the Camera Club of New York. A small group of photographers soon surrounded him, which included Clarence White, Gertrude Kasebier, Alvin Longedon Coburn, Edward Steichen, and others—all of whom became great and famous photographers in their own right. In 1902 the group broke away from the Camera Club and formed its own group, which Stieglitz named the Photo Secession. One year later Stieglitz published the first issue of *Camera Work,* a beautifully printed magazine that was devoted to promoting photography as an art form.

The new group met at 291 Fifth Avenue, in a room next to Edward Steichen's, where their photographs were displayed. The room, number 201, became the most famous locale of photography in the country.

The Photo Secessionists agreed on two fundamental principles: exploring new subject matter and concentrating on rendering the subtleties of light. Stieglitz believed a photograph should be straightforward, without manipulation on the paper surface, while others (like Steichen) believed the printing process should be controlled and manipulated. This same argument continues today.

In any event, *Camera Work* not only published the works of certain photographers, it was the means by which many European artists and writers were introduced to this country. The works of people such as Rodin, Matisse, John Marin, Gertrude Stein, Picasso, Brancusi, and Braque were published toward the end of *Camera Work*. In 1917, after alienating most of his fellow members by drastically reducing the number of photographs he published in *Camera Work*, Stieglitz was forced to close both the magazine and Gallery 291. However, Stieglitz succeeded in the promotion of photography as art. There is probably not a major museum in the world that does not exhibit photography.

There are many other great men in the history of photography, men whose contributions are almost immeasurable, such as the inventor Barnach, who was responsible for the pioneer 35mm. camera, the Leica, in 1924; the Lumiere brothers, who made the first successful color glass-plates for commercial use in 1907; and Mannes and Godowsky, two young musician-scientists at Kodak Laboratories, who introduced the first color roll film, Kodachrome, in 1935.

Whether photography is an art or a science, a hobby or therapy, does not matter in the end. Only the photograph is important—not who took it, or when it was made, or how it was done, or what camera was used. The photograph itself is man's most vital and important visual means for communicating ideas and thoughts to his fellow man.

Assignment: The History of Photography

1. Imagine that you are a photographer in the 1860s. You are traveling in some part of the world with the intention of documenting what you discover with photographs. What special problems would you have that you would not have today using modern equipment and film?

2. What is the difference in the appearance of the following photographic images?

    a. Daguerreotype   b. Ambrotype   c. Tintype

3. Which of the antique photographic processes was the forerunner of the negative-positive type processes in use today? In what way was this antique process different from today's method?

Appendix

GLOSSARY

Aberrations   Optical defects in a lens that limit the sharpness of the focused image.

Abrasions   Marks or scratches on the emulsion surface of photographic materials (usually film).

Acetate base   A support for photographic film usually composed of cellulose acetate.

Accelerator   The chemical ingredient in a developer solution that increases the activity of the reducing agent.

Acetic acid   A weak solution of acetic acid is used in stop baths to inhibit the action of the developer. It is also used in some fixing baths.

Agitation   The process used to bring fresh chemical solution in contact with photographic emulsion.

Air bubbles   Tiny bubbles of air that cling to the surface of an emulsion. They appear as black spots on a print. Sufficient agitation is usually recommended to prevent this from happening.

Antihalation backing   A coating on the backing of film that prevents reflections within the film.

Angle of view   A portion of a subject that is viewed by the lens on a camera. The angle of view is determined by the focal length of a lens.

Aperture   The opening in a lens system through which light passes. It is usually expressed as a fraction of the focal length, that is, f-stop.

A.S.A. (American Standards Association)   A standardized system for rating the light sensitivity of films.

Automatic camera   A camera with a built-in exposure meter that automatically adjusts the lens opening, shutter speed, or both.

Available light   The term usually implies an indoor or night time light condition of low intensity. It is also called "existing light."

Back   The portion of a camera that contains the film.

Back light   Illumination from a source behind the subject as seen from the position of the camera.

Base   See Acetate base.

Baseboard   The large board to which the enlarger column is attached. The enlarging easel is usually placed on the baseboard.

Bellows   The folding portion in some cameras that connects the lens to the camera body.

Between-the-lens shutter   A shutter designed to operate between two elements in a lens.

Bleach   Usually a solution that makes the silver salts in the print or film soluble in fixer. It can be used to remove all or part of the image.

Bleed   In a mounted photograph it refers to an image that extends to the boundaries of the board.

Blocked *or blocked up*   Refers to an area of a negative that is overexposed.

Blotter book   A number of sheets of blotting paper, interleaved with nonabsorbent tissue used to dry photographic papers.

Blue sensitive   The degree of color sensitivity of an ordinary silver emulsion to blue and ultraviolet wavelengths.

Bounce light   Light that is directed away from the subject toward a reflective surface.

Bracket To make a number of different exposures of the same subject in the same lighting conditions.

Bulb A marked setting (B) on some cameras that permits the shutter to stay open for an indefinite period by continued pressure on the shutter release.

Burning in The process of giving additional exposure to part of the image by an enlarger.

Cable release A flexible cord made out of cloth or metal that normally screws into a threaded socket on the shutter or camera body. When released, it will trip the shutter without camera movement.

Cadmium sulfide cell A photo-conductive light sensitive device used in some exposure meters.

Calotype A photographic process employing a negative image to produce a positive image. Invented by William Henry Fox Talbot around 1840.

Camera Latin meaning "room." The instrument with which photographs are taken.

Camera obscura Latin for "dark room." The camera obscura is the ancestor of the photographic camera. It was used by early painters as an aid for sketching.

Camera angles Various positions of the camera in relation to the subject, giving different effects or viewpoints.

Carrier The negative holder in an enlarger.

Cartridge A metal or plastic container in which film is held. Usually, it refers to the container for Instamatic-type film.

Cassette A metal or plastic container in which film is held. The cassette usually refers to the container for 35mm film.

CdS meter An exposure meter that uses a cadmium sulfide cell and is battery-operated.

Changing bag A light-tight bag with openings for the hands in which film can be loaded and unloaded in daylight.

Circle of confusion An optical term used to describe the size of an out-of-focus image point formed by a lens. The more out of focus an image is, the larger the circle of confusion.

Clearing agent A chemical that neutralizes hypo (fixer) in film or paper thus reducing washing time.

Close-up lens A supplementary lens that, when placed over a camera lens, shortens its focal length and allows a closer focusing distance.

Coating A thin film of magnesium fluoride, or other materials, that reduces the intensity of flare light within the lens, thus increasing the brightness and contrast of the image.

Cold tones Bluish or greenish tones in a black and white print.

Collodion Substance used to attach and suspend silver grains to a glass plate, used in the preparation of "wet plate" emulsion. Described by Frederick Scott Archer in 1851.

Color balance The ability of a film to realistically reproduce the colors of a scene. Color films are balanced in manufacture for light of certain color quality.

Color temperature A system established to determine the color of light. Color temperature is expressed in degrees Kelvin (K).

Composition The visual arrangement of all elements in a photograph.

Condenser lens An optical system of lenses used in many enlargers.

Contact paper A photographic printing paper used in contact printing.

Contact print A print made by exposing contact paper while it is held tightly against the negative.

Contrast The comparison of tonal values in a negative or print. A contrasty negative or print has few middle tones.

Contrast grade A number given to a particular printing paper. The range is normally 1-6 with 2 considered normal. The higher the number, the higher the contrast. Printing filters are numbered similarly.

Contrasty The condition where the range of tones is too great in a negative or print.

Cropping Selective use of a portion of an image recorded on a negative.

Cut film Film that is cut to various sizes (for example, 4x5, 8x10, etc.). Also known as sheet film.

Darkroom A light-tight area used for processing and handling light-sensitive materials.

Definition The impression of clarity of detail in the photograph.

Dense Darkness in a negative usually caused by overexposure or overdevelopment.

Densitometer An instrument for measuring the density of an area in a photographic image.

Density The blackness of an area in a negative or print that is determined by the amount of light that can pass through a negative or reflect from a print.

Depth of field The distance range between the nearest and farthest planes that appear in acceptably sharp focus in a photograph.

Depth of field scales A calibrated ring, chart, or scale, often engraved on a camera lens mount, on which the depth of field can be determined for any given distance and aperture.

Depth of focus The distance range over which the film can be shifted at the film plane inside the camera and still have the subject appear in sharp focus. This term is often confused with depth of field.

Developer A chemical solution used to make the latent image (invisible) become a visible image on exposed paper or film.

Developing tank A light-tight container used for processing film.

Developing out The photographic process by which a latent image is made visible by development.

Diaphragm A perforated plate or adjustable opening mounted behind or between the elements of a lens that controls the amount of light that reaches the film or paper. These openings are usually calibrated in f-numbers.

Diffraction The spreading of a light ray after it passes near the edge of an object.

Diffusion Scattered, indirect lighting that softens detail in a print. Usually achieved with a diffusion disc or glass in an enlarger.

DIN The German system of determining film speed.

Distortion Defects in the shape of an image caused by certain types of lenses, such as the curvature of lines with wide-angle lenses.

Dodging The practice of using an opaque material to lighten an area in a print.

Double exposure The recording of two separate images on a single negative or the printing of two separate images on a single sheet of photographic paper.

Drum dryer A machine used for drying paper prints.

Dry mounting A method of mounting prints on cardboard or similar materials by means of heat, pressure, and tissue impregnated with shellac.

Dry mounting press The machine used to dry mount photographs.

Dry mounting tissue A thin tissue paper, usually impregnated with shellac, which, when heated sufficiently will adhere a print to various materials.

Easel Holds photographic paper flat for exposure under the enlarger.

Electronic flash A repeatable flash produced by a high voltage electrical discharge in a glass tube filled with gas.

Element A single unit in the structure of a lens.

Emulsion A thin coating of light-sensitive material, usually silver halide in gelatin, in which the image is formed on film and photographic paper.

Emulsion side The side of the photographic material coated with the emulsion.

Enlargement A print that is larger than the negative. Also called blow-up.

Enlarger A device consisting of a light source, a negative carrier, and a lens, and a means of adjusting these to project an image from a negative to a sheet of photographic paper.

Exposure The quantity of light allowed to act on a light-sensitive material; a product of the intensity (controlled by the aperture size) and the duration (controlled by the shutter speed or enlarging time) of light striking the film or paper. Also used to describe the actual act of taking the picture.

Exposure latitude The range of camera exposures, from underexposure to overexposure which will produce an acceptable negative.

Exposure meter An instrument used to measure light and to equate that information into the appropriate shutter speed and aperture setting.

Exposure setting The lens opening and shutter speed selected to expose the film.

Fading The deterioration of the print image over a period of time.

Farmer's reducer A compound containing potassium ferricyanide and sodium thiosulfate, used to reduce negative densities.

Fast A term used to describe films of high sensitivity or lenses of large apertures.

Ferrotype Originally a name for the tintype process popular from the 1860s to 1880s.

Ferrotype plates (tins) Sheets of highly polished stainless steel, tin, or chromium plated metal used to dry prints to a high gloss finish.

Film The light-sensitive material used for exposure, generally in a camera.

Film clips Spring clips that hold the film securely at one end.

Film speed The relative sensitivity of the film to light. Rated usually in ASA numbers. (See A.S.A.)

Filter A colored piece of glass or other transparent material used over the lens to emphasize, eliminate, or change the density or color of the subject or a portion of the subject.

Filter factor The number by which the correct exposure without the filter must be multiplied to obtain the same relative exposure with the filter.

Fisheye lens A type of wide-angle lens, or lens attachment, capable of covering a field of 180° or more.

Fixed-focus lens A lens that has been focused in a fixed position by the manufacturer.

Fixing bath A solution that makes film or paper insensitive to further exposure to light. Usually contains hypo.

Flash A brief, intense burst of light produced by a flashbulb or an electronic flash unit.

Flashing A method of darkening an area of a print by exposing it to white light prior to the fixing bath.

Flat A term used to describe a low contrast negative or print.

Flat lighting Lighting the subject in such a way as to produce a minimum of shadows and contrast in the subject.

Flood A photographic light source designed to illuminate a wide area.

F-number A number used to designate the size and light-passing ability of the lens opening on most adjustable cameras. The larger the f-number, the smaller the lens opening. F-numbers are fractions of the focal length.

Focal length The distance from the lens to a point behind the lens (focal point) where the light rays are in focus when the distance is set at infinity.

Focal plane The plane where the image is brought into a critical focus. In a camera, the film is placed at the focal plane.

Focal plane shutter An opaque curtain shutter containing a slit that moves directly in front of the film in a camera.

Focus To adjust the distance scale on a camera so that the image is sharp on the focal plane.

Fog Darkening or discoloring of a negative or print caused by extraneous light or chemical action. Can also be caused by using outdated film or storing the film in a hot, humid condition.

Foreground The area between the camera and the main subject.

Frontlighting Light falling on the subject from in front of the subject.

Gelatin The material most often used in photographic emulsions to suspend the silver salts.

Glossy Used to describe a printing paper with a smooth surface which can be used for ferrotyping. The print has a mirror-like finish.

Graduate A container which is calibrated in fluid ounces or milliliters used in measuring liquid photographic chemicals.

Grain The individual silver particles or groups of particles in the emulsion layer, which when enlarged, become visible.

Gray card A card of known reflectance, usually 18%, used to determine the exposure.

Ground glass A name for a type of focusing screen in a camera.

Halation A blur, or halo effect, that sometimes occurs around a bright subject.

Halides Metallic compound that contains the light-sensitive materials upon which most photographic processes are based.

Hard A term used to describe an image that is high in contrast.

Hardener A chemical that is added to the fixing bath to harden the gelatin after development.

Highlights The brightest areas on a print and the darkest areas in a negative.

Hyperfocal distance The distance from the camera to the near plane of the depth of field when the lens is focused at infinity.

Hypo Chemical used in fixing baths to make soluble the undeveloped silver salts in an emulsion and to stop the action of the developer.

Hypo eliminator A bath for films and papers. It is intended to shorten washing times. In reality, hypo eliminator does not eliminate hypo but aids in its removal.

Image The visual result of the exposure and development on a photographic emulsion.

Incident light The light reaching the subject from all sources.

Incident meter A meter designed to read incident light.

Infinity In photography, the distance from the camera beyond which no further focusing adjustment is required to maintain a sharp image.

Infrared Light rays which are invisible with ordinary films past the red end of the visible spectrum.

Intensifier A chemical solution used to increase the density (contrast) of a photographic image.

Interchangeable lens A lens which can be removed from a camera body.

Iris diaphragm See Diaphragm.

Latent image The invisible image left by the action of light on photographic materials.

Leaf shutter A type of shutter consisting of a number of thin blades or leaves installed between the lens components (elements) or behind the lens.

Lens One or more pieces of optical glass, plastic, or other material, designed to collect and focus light rays to form a sharp image on the film or paper.

Lens barrel The metal tube in which the lens is mounted.

Lens board A wooden or metal panel on which a lens is mounted to an enlarger or view camera.

Lens hood An accessory used to shield the lens from extraneous light. Also called lens shade.

Lens mount A portion on a camera which holds the lens to the body.

Lens tissue A soft, lintless tissue used for cleaning lenses.

Light meter See Exposure meter.

Long lens A lens whose focal length is longer than the diagonal measurement of the film. Generally used to describe telephoto lenses.

Macro lens A special type of lens used for photographing subjects at close ranges.

Matte Used to describe a finish on paper—nonglossy or dull.

Maximum aperture The largest opening on a lens.

M, F, X Marking found on many shutters to indicate the flash synchronization. M is for medium peak flash bulbs, F denotes fast peak flash bulbs, X used for electronic flash.

Micro prism A type of focusing aid found in many ground glass viewing screens. It usually consists of a pattern of dots.

Negative Any photographic image in which the subject tones have been reversed. Usually, it refers to film.

Negative carrier The frame which holds the negative in an enlarger.

Normal lens Any lens whose focal length is approximately equal to the diagonal measurement of the film being exposed through it.

Opaque Incapable of transmitting light. Also a commercial product which is painted on a negative to black out an area.

Orthochromatic A type of emulsion which is sensitive to visible blue and green but not to red.

Overexposure A condition in which too much light was allowed to reach the film. It produces a dense negative.

Panchromatic An emulsion which is sensitive to blue, green, and most of the red regions of the spectrum.

Paper The light-sensitive paper used in making prints.

Paper negative A negative image on a paper base.

Parallax In photography, the difference between the field of view seen through the viewfinder and that recorded on the film.

Photoflood A photographic light source.

Photogram An image made by placing objects on a sheet of photographic paper and exposing it to light.

Photomicrography Photography through a microscope.

Pinhole camera A camera that has a pinhole aperture in place of a lens.

Pinholes Tiny transparent spots in the negative caused by the developer not reaching the film.

Polarized light Waves of light which vibrate uniformly in, or parallel to, a particular plane.

Polarizer A filter or screen which transmits polarized light.

Positive An image in which the tones are similar to those of the subject. A print made from a negative.

Primary colors of light Any one of the three colors of light that make white light—red, blue or green.

Primary pigment colors A mixture of the primary pigment colors—magenta, yellow, and cyan—produces black.

Print An image, usually positive, on photographic paper.

Printing out A method of photographic printing, where the visible image is formed by the action of light, rather than being developed-out.

Projection print Refers to any print made by projection usually with an enlarger.

Rangefinder An optical-mechanical device consisting of a system of lenses and prisms. When installed in a viewfinder of a camera, it will visually show the out-of-focus image.

Rangefinder camera A camera with a built-in rangefinder.

Reciprocity law A law which states that exposure varies uniformly with changes in either time or intensity (exposure).

Reducer agent A chemical solution used to decrease the overall density of a negative.

Reflected meter An exposure meter which measures the light reflected by the subject.

Reflector Any surface used to reflect light.

Reflex camera A kind of camera in which the viewfinder image is formed by the lens and reflected by an inclined mirror onto a ground glass.

Refraction The bending of light rays as they pass obliquely from one medium to another medium of different density.

Replenisher A chemical solution designed to restore the strength and capacity of a developer.

Reticulation The cracking or distorting of the emulsion during processing usually caused by wide temperature or chemical-activity differences between the solutions.

Roll film Film supplied in rolls rather than sheets. Usually used to describe those films protected from light by paper leaders.

Safelight Illumination in a darkrom that will not normally expose photo sensitive material.

Self-timer A device that is either attached or built in a camera to allow a time delay before the shutter is released.

Sensitivity The susceptibility of an emulsion to the energy of light.

Sepia toning A chemical process which converts the blackened silver image to a brownish image.

Sheet film See Cut film.

Short lens Any lens whose focal length is shorter than the diagonal measurement of the film. Also called wide-angle lens.

Shutter The device which opens and closes to admit light to the film.

Shutter release The lever which allows the shutter to operate. Also called the trigger.

Shutter speed The duration of the exposure. Also, the marked settings on a shutter dial.

Single-lens reflex A type of camera that allows viewing through the picture-taking lens. This is accomplished with the use of a mirror. Abbrev. as SLR.

Slow A term that denotes a long shutter speed. Can also be applied to a relatively insensitive film.

Soft Used to describe a print or negative which is low in contrast. Also used to describe an image which is not sharp.

Spectrum The colored bands of light formed by the dispersion of white light as it passes through a prism.

Spotting The process of bleaching or painting out spots or defects from a negative or print.

Spotting colors The colors used in spotting.

Stop bath A chemical solution which neutralizes the developer.

Stock solution Photographic chemicals in concentrated form. Intended to be diluted with water for use.

Stop down To reduce the size of the lens opening.

Supplementary lens A lens or lens system intended to be used over a camera lens to alter the effective focal length. Such a lens can allow closer than normal focusing distance.

Tacking iron A tool used to attach dry mounting tissue to the print or board.

Taking lens The lens which forms the image on the film in a twin-lens reflex camera. The other lens is for viewing and framing the subject.

Tank A light-tight container made of plastic or metal in which the film is placed for processing.

Telephoto lens See Long lenses.

Test print A piece of photographic paper which is exposed to a sequence of regular and cumulative exposures to determine the correct exposure for a particular negative on that type of paper.

Thin Denotes a negative of low density.

Time A marking on many shutters (T). When the shutter is set on T and released, it will remain open until it is released again.

Time exposure Refers to an exposure longer than 1 second.

Tonal scale The range of grays (densities) in a photographic image.

Toning A chemical method for changing the color or tone of a photographic image.

Translucent A diffusing material such as frosted glass, which will transmit light, but not focus light.

Transparency A photographic image which is viewed by translucent light. Usually, a color positive (slide).

Tray A shallow container, usually rectangular in which prints and films are processed.

Tripod A three-legged stand or support on which a camera can be attached. They are usually adjustable in height and provide a means of tilting the camera.

TTL Through-the-lens, refers to light meters built behind the camera lens.

Tungsten light Artificial illumination as opposed to daylight.

Ultraviolet Rays which comprise the invisible portion of the spectrum just beyond the visible violet.

Variable contrast paper A type of photographic paper that by the use of variable contrast filters, will change contrast of the paper.

Viewing lens The lens in which the subject is seen in a twin-lens reflex camera.

Warm tones The shades of red and orange (brown) in a black and white image.

Washed out Denotes a pale, overall gray print lacking highlights.

Weight Refers to the thickness of photographic paper.

Wide-angle See Short focal length lenses.

Working solution Chemical solution mixed from the stock solution.

Zoom lens A type of lens with a range of various focal lengths.

Bibliography

Books by and about Photographers

Adams, Ansel.
Singular Images. Hastings-on-Hudson, N. Y.: Morgan & Morgan, 1974.
Ansel Adams. Hastings-on-Hudson, N. Y.: Morgan & Morgan, 1972.

Arbus, Diane.
Diane Arbus: An Aperture Monograph. Millerton, N. Y.: Aperture, 1972.

Atget, Eugene.
The World of Atget, by Berenice Abbot. New York: Horizon Press, 1964.

Brandt, Bill.
Perspective of Nudes. Garden City, N. Y.: Amphoto, 1961.
Shadow of Light. New York: Viking Press, 1966.

Brady, Mathew.
Mathew Brady: Historian with a Camera, by James D. Hornan, New York: Bonanza, 1960.

Brassaï.
Brassaï. New York: Museum of Modern Art, 1968.

Bullock, Wynn.
Photography: A Way of Light. Hastings-on-Hudson, New York: Morgan & Morgan, 1973.

Cameron, Julia Margaret.
Julia Margaret Cameron. Millerton, N. Y.: Aperture, 1974.

Carroll, Lewis.
Lewis Carroll, Photographer, by Helmut Gernsheim. New York: Dover Publications, 1969.

Caponigro, Paul.
Paul Caponigro (An Aperture Monograph). Millerton, N. Y.: Aperture, 1967.

Callahan, Harry
Harry Callahan. New York: Museum of Modern Art, 1967.

Cartier-Bresson, Henri.
The Decisive Moment. New York: Simon & Schuster, 1952.
Photographs by Henri Cartier-Bresson. New York: Grossman, 1963.
The World of Henri Cartier-Bresson. New York: Viking, 1968.

Cunningham, Imogen.
Imogen! Photographs 1910-1973. Seattle: University of Washington Press, 1974.

Davidson, Bruce.
East 100th Street. Cambridge, Mass.: Harvard University Press, 1970.

Evans, Walker.
Message from the Interior. New York: The Eakins Press, 1966.
Let Us Now Praise Famous Men, James Agee. New York: Ballantine Books, 1972.

Frank, Robert.
The Americans. Millerton, N. Y.: Aperture, 1969.

Hine, Lewis W.
Lewis W. Hine, edited by Judith Gutman. New York: Grossman, 1974.

Jackson, William H.
William H. Jackson, by Beaumont Newhall and Diana E. Edkins. Hastings-on-Hudson, N. Y.: Morgan & Morgan, 1974.

Karsh, Yousuf.
In Search of Greatness. New York: Knopf, 1962.
Karsh Portfolio. Toronto, Canada: University of Toronto Press, 1967.

Kertesz, Andre.
Andre Kertesz, Photographer. New York: Museum of Modern Art, 1964.
Andre Kertesz: 60 Years of Photography 1912-1972. New York: Grossman, 1972.

Lange, Dorothea.
Dorothea Lange. New York: Museum of Modern Art, 1966.

Laughlin, Clarence John.
The Personal Eye. Millerton, N. Y.: Aperture, 1973.

Lartigue, J. H.
Boyhood Photos of J. H. Lartigue. Lausanne: Ami Guichard, 1966.
Les femmes. New York: E. P. Dutton, 1974.

Lyon, Danny.
Conversations with the Dead. New York: Holt, Rinehart & Winston, 1971.

Moholy-Nagy, Laszlo.
Painting, Photography, Film. Cambridge, Mass.: M.I.T. Press, 1973.

Penn, Irving.
Worlds in a Small Room. New York: Grossman, 1974.

Porter, Eliot.
In Wildness is the Preservation of the World. A Sierra Club Book. New York: Ballantine Books, 1967.

Smith, Eugene W.
W. Eugene Smith (An Aperture Monograph). Millerton, N. Y.: Aperture, 1969.

Siskind, Aaron.
Aaron Siskind: Photographer. Rochester, N.Y.: George Eastman House, 1965.

Steichen, Edward.
A Life in Photography. Garden City, N.Y.: Doubleday, 1963.

Stieglitz, Alfred.
An American Seer, by Dorothy Norman. Millerton, N. Y.: Aperture, 1973.

Strand, Paul.
Paul Strand (An Aperture Book), Vols. I & II, Millerton, N. Y.: Aperture, 1972.

Uelsmann, Jerry N.
Jerry N. Uelsmann (An Aperture Monograph). Millerton, N. Y.: Aperture, 1970.

Vroman, Adam Clark.
Dwellers at the Source, by William Webb and Robert A. Weinstein. New York: Grossman, 1973.

Weston, Edward.
My Camera on Point Lobos. New York: DaCapo, 1968.
Edward Weston: Photographer (An Aperture Monograph). Millerton, N. Y.: Aperture, 1965.
The Daybooks of Edward Weston, Vols. I and II. Millerton, N. Y.: Aperture, 1973.

Selected Books on Photography

History

Friedman, Joseph S. *History of Color Photography.* London: Focal Press Limited, 1968.

Gernsheim, Helmut. *A Concise History of Photography.* New York: Grosset and Dunlap, 1965.

——— *The History of Photography.* New York: Oxford University Press, 1955.

——— *Creative Photography: Aesthetic Trends 1839–1960.* Farber & Farber, 1962.

——— *L. J. M. Daguerre, The History of the Daguerreotype.* New York: Dover Publications, 1968.

Mess, C. E. Kenneth. *From Dry Plates to Ektachrome Film: A Story of Photographic Research.* New York: Ziff-Davis, 1961.

Newhall, Beaumont. *The History of Photography from 1839 to the Present Day.* New York: Museum of Modern Art, 1964.

——— *Latent Image: The Discovery of Photography.* Garden City, N.Y.: Doubleday, 1967.

——— *The Daguerreotype in America.* Greenwich, Conn.: New York Graphic Society, Ltd., 1968.

Pollack, Peter. *The Picture History of Photography from the Earliest Beginnings to the Present Day.* New York: Harry Abrams, 1969.

Rinehart, Floyd and Marion. *American Daguerrian Art.* New York: Crown Publishers, Inc. 1967.

Rudisill, Richard. *Mirror Image, The Influence of the Daguerreotype on American Society.* Albuquerque: University of New Mexico Press, 1971.

Taft, Robert. *Photography and the American Scene, A Social History, 1839–1889.* New York: Dover Publications, 1964.

Wall, E. J. *The History of Three-Color Photography.* London: Focal Press Limited, 1970.

Technical Books

Adventures in Existing Light, AC–44. New York: Eastman Kodak Co.

Applied Infrared Photography, M–28. New York: Eastman Kodak Co.

Artificial-Light Photography, by Ansel Adams. Hastings-on-Hudson, N.Y.: Morgan & Morgan, 1971.

Basic Color Photography, by Andreas Feininger. Garden City, N.Y.: Amphoto, 1972.

The Camera, by the Editors of Time-Life Books. Hastings-on-Hudson, N.Y.: Morgan & Morgan, 1970.

Camera & Lens—The Creative Approach, by Ansel Adams. Hastings-on-Hudson, N.Y.: Morgan & Morgan, 1970.

Close-Up Photography, Vol. I, N-12A. New York: Eastman Kodak Co.

Close-Up Photography, Vol. II, N-12B. New York: Eastman Kodak Co.

Copying, M-1. New York: Eastman Kodak Co.

The Creative Photographer, by Andreas Feininger. Englewood Cliffs, N.J.: Prentice-Hall, 1975.

Darkroom Techniques, by Andreas Feininger. New York: Amphoto, 1974.

Dictionary of Contemporary Photography, by Hollis N. Todd and Leslie Stroebel. Hastings-on-Hudson, N.Y.: Morgan & Morgan, 1974.

Discover Yourself through Photography, by Ralph Hattersley. Hastings-on-Hudson, N.Y.: Morgan & Morgan, 1971.

Filters, A-B-1. New York: Eastman Kodak Co.

The Hole Thing—A Manual of Pinhole Fotography, by Jim Shull. Hastings-on-Hudson, N.Y.: Morgan & Morgan, 1974.

Kodak Black-and-White Photographic Papers, G-1. New York: Eastman Kodak Co.

Kodak Color Films, E-77. New York: Eastman Kodak Co.

Kodak Darkroom Data Guide, R-20. New York: Eastman Kodak Co.

Kodak Master Photoguide, AR-21. New York: Eastman Kodak Co.

Kodak Professional Black-and-White Films, F-5. New York: Eastman Kodak Co.

Kodak Professional Photoguide R-28. New York: Eastman Kodak Co.

Leica Manual, edited by Douglas O. Morgan, David Vestal, William Broecker. Hastings-on-Hudson, N.Y.: Morgan & Morgan, 1973.

Natural-light Photography, by Ansel Adams. Hastings-on-Hudson, N.Y.: Morgan & Morgan, 1971.

The Negative, by Ansel Adams. Hastings-on-Hudson, N.Y.: Morgan & Morgan, 1972.

Photo-lab Index, edited by Ernest M. Pittaro. Hastings-on-Hudson, N.Y.: Morgan & Morgan, 1975.

Photography with Large-Format Cameras O-18. New York: Eastman Kodak Co.

Photography through the Microscope P-2. New York: Eastman Kodak Co.

Photographic Filters, by Leslie Stroebel. Hastings-on-Hudson, N.Y.: Morgan & Morgan, 1974.

Photographic Lenses, by C. B. Nesbett. Hastings-on-Hudson, N.Y.: Morgan & Morgan, 1973.

Photographic Sensitometry: The Study of Tone Reproduction, by Hollis N. Todd and Richard D. Zakia. Hastings-on-Hudson, N.Y.: Morgan & Morgan, 1969.

Photographic Literature, 1960–1970, Vol. 2, by Albert Boni. Hastings-on-Hudson, N.Y.: Morgan & Morgan, 1970.

Practical Sensitometry, by George L. Wafefield. Hastings-on-Hudson, N.Y.: Morgan & Morgan, 1970.

The Print, by Ansel Adams. Hastings-on-Hudson, N.Y.: Morgan & Morgan, 1971.

Processing Chemicals and Formulas J-1. New York: Eastman Kodak Co.

Professional Portrait Techniques 0-4. New York: Eastman Kodak Co.

Special Problems, by the editors of Time-Life Books. Hastings-on-Hudson, N.Y.: Morgan & Morgan, 1971.

Zone System Manual, by Minor White. Hastings-on-Hudson, N.Y.: Morgan & Morgan, 1972.

Collections

Art of Photography, by the editors of Time-Life Books. Hastings-on-Hudson, N.Y.: Morgan & Morgan, 1971.

Concerned Photographer 2, edited by Cornell Capa. New York: Grossman, 1973.

Documentary Photography, by the editors of Time-Life Books. Hastings-on-Hudson, N.Y.: Morgan & Morgan, 1972.

The Family of Man, edited by Edward Steichen. New York: Museum of Modern Art, 1955.

French Primitive Photography. Millerton, N.Y.: Aperture, 1970.

Frontiers of Photography, by the editors of Time-Life Books. Hastings-on-Hudson, N.Y.: Morgan & Morgan, 1972.

The Great Photographers, by the editors of Time-Life Books. Hastings-on-Hudson, N.Y.: Morgan & Morgan, 1971.

Great Themes, by the editors of Time-Life Books. Hastings-on-Hudson, N.Y.: Morgan & Morgan, 1970.

Looking at Photographs, edited by John Szarkowski. New York: Museum of Modern Art, 1973.

Photographers on Photography, edited by Nathan Lyons. Englewood Cliffs, N.J.: Prentice-Hall, 1966.

Woman's Eye, by Anne Tucker. New York: Knopf, 1973.

Career Books

Careers in Photography, by Edna Bennett. New York: Amphoto, 1962.

Cash from Your Camera, by Louis Peek. Hastings,on-Hudson, N.Y.: Morgan & Morgan, 1970.

How & Where to Sell Your Pictures Overseas, by Ahlers & Webb. New York: Amphoto, 1963.

Photography for Fun & Profit. Career Institute Staff.

Photography Game, by Arthur Goldsmith. New York: Viking Press, 1971.

Photo Marketplace. How and Where to Sell Your Photos, by Thomas Kovarik and John Hurst. Hastings-on-Hudson, N.Y.: Morgan & Morgan, 1973.

The Professional Photographer in Practice, by Robert P. Hymers. Hastings-on-Hudson, N.Y.: Morgan & Morgan, 1969.

Magazines

Aperture. Aperture Inc., New York.

British Journal of Photography. Henry Greenwood & Co., London.

Camera. C. J. Bucher Ltd. Lucerne, Switzerland.

Camera 35. U.S. Camera Publishing Co., New York.

Infinity. American Society of Magazine Photographers, New York.

Modern Photography. Billboard Publishing Co., New York.

Popular Photography. Ziff-Davis Publishing Co., New York.

U.S. Camera World Annual. U.S. Camera Publishing Corp., New York.

photography in focus

JACQUELINE OSTER
COORDINATOR OF ART
SCHOOL DISTRICT 19K